# Created
### for a
# Purpose

## DARLENE & BONNIE SALA

# BARBOUR BOOKS
An Imprint of Barbour Publishing, Inc.

© 2020 by Darlene Sala and Bonnie Sala

Print ISBN 978-1-64352-451-1

eBook Editions:
Adobe Digital Edition (.epub) 978-1-64352-587-7
Kindle and MobiPocket Edition (.prc) 978-1-64352-588-4

All scripture quotations, unless otherwise indicated, are taken from the HOLY BIBLE, NEW INTERNATIONAL VERSION®. NIV®. Copyright © 1973, 1978, 1984, 2011 by Biblica, Inc.™ Used by permission. All rights reserved worldwide.

Scripture quotations marked EBR are taken from the Rotherham Emphasized Bible.

Scripture quotations marked NKJV are taken from the New King James Version®. Copyright © 1982 by Thomas Nelson, Inc. Used by permission. All rights reserved.

Scripture quotations marked TLB are taken from The Living Bible © 1971 by Tyndale House Foundation. Used by permission of Tyndale House Publishers, Inc., Carol Stream, Illinois 60188. All rights reserved.

Scriptures marked ASV are taken from the American Standard Version of the Bible.

Scripture quotations marked NLT are taken from the *Holy Bible*. New Living Translation copyright© 1996, 2004, 2015 by Tyndale House Foundation. Used by permission of Tyndale House Publishers, Inc. Carol Stream, Illinois 60188. All rights reserved.

Scripture quotations marked MSG are from *THE MESSAGE*. Copyright © by Eugene H. Peterson 1993, 1994, 1995, 1996, 2000, 2001, 2002. Used by permission of NavPress Publishing Group.

Scripture quotations marked ESV are from The Holy Bible, English Standard Version®, copyright © 2001 by Crossway Bibles, a publishing ministry of Good News Publishers. Used by permission. All rights reserved.

Scripture quotations marked PHILLIPS are from The New Testament in Modern English by J.B Phillips copyright © 1960, 1972 J. B. Phillips. Administered by The Archbishops' Council of the Church of England. Used by Permission.

Published by Barbour Books, an imprint of Barbour Publishing, Inc., 1810 Barbour Drive, Uhrichsville, Ohio 44683 www.barbourbooks.com

*Our mission is to inspire the world with the life-changing message of the Bible.*

Member of the
Evangelical Christian
Publishers Association

Printed in the United States of America.

## DEDICATED TO

*Darlene's "Next-Door Bible Study Gals,"*
*with special love to Sandi*
*Bonnie's "Step-Sisters": Carolyn, Dana, Cindy,*
*Raylene, Eileen, Sarah, Vikki, Kathy D, Maria,*
*Pam & Kathy K. We are so much better together!*
*And to Karissa. We'll be reading her books one day.*

# CONTENTS

# INTRODUCTION

It's been more than twenty years since I wrote the original edition of *Created for a Purpose*! So why this new edition now? So much in the world has changed for women—and nothing has changed. I have written with my daughter Bonnie because Bonnie has lived through much of that change. As she wrote, she worked with a focus group of women who are starting out in life.

Yes, cultures have changed immensely—yet many of the issues women face and the cries of our hearts remain the same. Women still need to know they were *created for a purpose*.

A little phenomenon called *social media* now has a huge impact on us. Where the options in a woman's life were relatively limited, now most of us are in the workforce to help put food on the table and we're cultivating careers. But we still face limitations; we're stretched way too thin and we so often do not feel *enough*.

Together, Bonnie and I pray this book will help lead you to your purpose and the One who gives you worth.

*Darlene*

# CHAPTER 1

## Navigating the Pain That Is Life

### Why You Need to Know Who and Whose You Are

*My husband left me for another man's wife
and married her. We were married for twenty-
nine and one-half years. My children—five
of them—and I had no idea he felt the way he
did. Three months before he asked me for a
divorce, I got a card in the mail from him
signed, "To the best wife in the whole
world—all my love forever." My whole life
has changed—upside down and inside out.
Pain—I have never felt so much pain. I almost killed myself. I wish I could close my eyes
and wake up and find this is all a bad dream.*

Can't you just feel the anguish in this woman's
message?

We talk with and hear from women all over

the world. Of course, we love hearing from people whose lives have been changed by hearing what God says about them in His Word, the Bible. These are women who have acted on what they heard and have seen their lives transformed. Our hearts are lifted by these stories of faith and redemption.

But many of the messages we receive are not great reads. Some, like the one above, are filled with heartache; some come from women who are enduring more problems than anyone should have to deal with in one lifetime. These women have fallen into a pit so deep that they can no longer see even a tiny sunlit circle above them.

One woman was in such despair that she was considering taking her own life. Her letter was a cry for help that couldn't be ignored.

> *I just heard your five-minute talk on suicide.*
> *I have spent most of the night weighing the*
> *pros and cons of suicide. The depression just*
> *won't leave. I can't stand it any longer.*
> *Medicine doesn't help. All I do is cry. Where is*

*God? Please send the book you mentioned.*
*I only hope I'll still be here when it comes.*

Not all the messages that come to us are this dramatic, but they all touch the heart. Some are from mothers so burdened with caring for their little ones and trying to make ends meet that they feel their lives count for nothing. They have no time for anything but their daily struggle for survival, and that struggle has buried their identities. Not only do they fail to see or feel God's presence with them, they may not know or may have lost all sense of their worth in God's eyes.

*It is the middle of the night, and here I am writing to you. I am supposed to be trusting in Jesus. Today I look to Him, but I find no comfort. What is bothering me is me—who am I? I am only nineteen. My mother and father are gone. I am the last of nine children. I have two children I love, and they're all I have to live for. Please write me back.*

In reality, all of us suffer in one way or another in this life. Those we love betray us; we suffer unexpected loss, illness strikes, and unrelenting hopelessness takes hold of our lives. God seems far away. Some of us will survive and rebuild our lives. Others will only fall deeper and deeper into despair.

What makes the difference? Our experience has been that a woman who understands what God says about her navigates the pain in her life differently. If you live a life with a real sense of who you are and Whose you are, you have resources beyond yourself. You have something called God's grace, which makes all the difference.

Most women, however, tend to get their sense of identity and sense of worth from three sources: their accomplishments, their appearance, and their relationships. Unfortunately, as we'll discuss later, all of these are susceptible to change. No matter how talented we are, some of our efforts will fail; illness and aging have their ways; and one way or another, even the best and most loving relationship comes to an end in this world.

There is good news though. As women, our

identities and self-worth do not need to be dependent on any of these things. We have an identity and worth of inestimable value that comes from a source that never changes. We can each come to know our value in God's eyes. "The king's daughter within the palace is all glorious," says Psalm 45:13 (asv). Through Jesus Christ, we can become daughters of the King and truly glorious in God's eyes through the transforming power of His Son.

Steve Arterburn, founder and chairman of New Life Ministries, says that the goal of secular counseling is to make you feel *good* about yourself, but the goal of biblical counseling is to make you feel *right* about yourself. That is also the goal of this book. It is written specifically for women because we struggle with who we are and what gives us value in very different ways and, arguably, more so than men. The most heartbreaking letters we've received come from women.

This is not to say that men feel better about themselves just because they are men. From childhood, men are conditioned to act, not feel. We know that in truth they *do* feel, but what we see are their actions, not their pain. To a man, emotional pain is something to be swallowed down and denied. Sometimes even their wives never suspect that they are suffering. Achievement of any kind brings a sense of worth, and if there is one thing men are taught today, it's to achieve in the world, to beat out the next guy, and prove their worth in their day-to-day lives through their actions, not their feelings.

Women, on the other hand, are conditioned to care for others, to be supportive, and to see themselves in terms of their relationships with others. The most successful married, professional woman is still expected to keep her children in clean clothing, have weekly date nights with her husband, stay fit, get along with everyone in the office or in her community, and contribute to the lives of others in her "spare time." If she is capable of doing all this with grace, good humor, and love, others will respect her, and their respect will build her self-esteem.

Can you see how this leaves women with the short end of the stick? A man is allowed more latitude in his personal and professional life. If he is an achiever, he will be respected and esteemed regardless of the fact that he treats others horribly and has dismal interpersonal skills. Women, on the other hand, must be pleasant and nurturing while they achieve. Sarah, a thirty-two-year-old real estate manager, says that "We, as women, are expected and raised to be sweet, kind, loving, gentle, caring, etc., which are all great qualities, but there is also the expectation that we will take a backseat, be soft-spoken, allow a man to be a leader first, and to stand by his side."

A woman's success is often tied to how others see her. But if your sense of worth depends on what others think of you, you have no control over that. It's often not enough to do a job well; a highly successful woman will be discredited if she's not liked by others. You may be tired and struggling today, trying to figure out who you really are, with an incorrect sense of your own worth. Maybe this is camouflaged as an eating disorder, drinking, compulsive shopping, depression, fear, obsession with your appearance, your online social presence, or by one of several other behaviors.

We may act out, make terrible decisions, and

allow ourselves to be treated horribly without knowing who we are, Whose we are, and why we are alive. These behaviors merely signal the existence of an underlying problem. We must deal with their cause, not just slap on a bandage and ignore the infection. If we did that, the problem would just break out in a different set of symptoms.

If you are struggling with these issues, we would like to give you hugs and remind you that God loves you—that you are valuable to Him, and He made you as the very expression of His beauty.

While you won't find specific advice in this book on these painful individual problems, we hope to give you a basis—a foundation—for understanding your worth, no matter what your gifts, life story, flaws, or limitations. You may need additional help or counseling to deal with a specific issue, but in order to build a lasting sense of who you are and just what you are worth, first you need a good foundation, one based not on what you *do* but who you *are*. No, you may not feel good about yourself every day, but if you see yourself as God sees you, you can feel *right* about yourself every day. You'll know you are a person of worth to God and that He is working in you to bring you a rich and satisfying life through His Son, Jesus, and to show His glory through you.

Aimee Lee Ball recalls a scene from the movie "Pretty Woman":

> *It occurred to me that plenty of us have the same self-doubt that derailed the Julia Roberts character. There's a scene where she's telling the wealthy businessman played by Richard Gere that nobody ever plans to be a hooker, that she fell into this line of work because she didn't think much of herself. Gere observes that she's a special person with a lot of potential and capabilities. And she replies, "The bad stuff is easier to believe."[1]*

So, let's get started on just exactly what God says about you.

---

[1] Aimee Lee Ball, "Women and the Negativity Receptor," O, The Oprah Magazine, August 8, 2008, https://www.oprah.com/omagazine/why-women-have-low-self-esteem-how-to-feel-more-confident/all.

# EMBRACING THE WORD

*"I have come that they may have life,*
*and have it to the full."*
JOHN 10:10

Jesus doesn't want you to have a pinched, skinny lit-tle life, a life that's constricted by doubts and fears about your own worth. No, He wants you to have a life that's full and rich. That's what this Bible verse from the Gospel of John is saying: Jesus wants you to really *live*. People who don't know Christ tend to think that the life He offers is one that's full of legalistic rules and restrictions. But Jesus loves you so much that He came to earth and died so that, through Him, you could have a real life, a full life forever.

Jesus' approach to women and His interaction with them was nothing short of revolutionary in His day. "Out of a cultural background that min-imized the dignity of women and even deperson-alized them, Jesus boldly affirmed their worth and gladly benefited from their vital ministry. He made the unusual practice of speaking freely to women, and in public no less (John 4:27; 8:10-11; Luke 7:12-13)."[2]

He came for women, just as much as He did for men. If you read through the Gospels, which tell the story of Jesus' time here, you'll notice how many of the stories have to do with women. Jesus never failed to reach out with love and compassion and healing to every woman He met. He came to earth especially for everyone whom the world ignores, for everyone who suffers under a heavy load, for everyone who feels worthless and wounded.

We can be sure that when He said, "I have come that they may have life and have it to the full," we are included in the great purpose for which He came to earth. He came to redeem and restore us all forever so that we can have a life that is full and rich, unobstructed by doubts and fears. He came to earth and gave Himself as a sacrifice so that you could be reconciled to God and have a real life, a full life—forever.

Jesus is reaching out to you today with the same compassionate love. He wants to heal your wounded

[2] Kevin DeYoung, "Our Pro-Woman, Complementarian Jesus," TGC, February 15, 2016, https://www.thegospelcoalition.org/article/our-pro-woman-complementarian-jesus/.

places. You are precious to Him. When you look to Him and what He says about you, you will find freedom from all doubts about your own worth. He wants you to live life to its fullest.

## GOING FURTHER. . .

1. What makes you feel good about yourself?
2. List some of the ways that you see women acting out because of a poor sense of self-worth.
3. When you look at your own life, do you see any of these behaviors?

Whenever you look in the mirror this week, remind yourself, "I am precious to Jesus."

*Sometimes, God, I feel as though I can't do anything right. I try so hard, but I never can do all the things I feel I should. Something's always left undone, or else it's done but not very well! I get so frustrated and discouraged sometimes that I just want to give up. Times like these, I don't like myself very much. Dear God, help me to turn to*

*You whenever I feel like this. Remind me that I can feel right about myself even on the days when I don't feel good about myself. Thank You for loving me so much that You sent Jesus. Thank You for the full, abundant life You offer me. Amen.*

# CHAPTER 2

## The Worth of a Woman

### Our Values and God's Values

*[W]omen have been engaged in intense, public hand-wringing dialogues with themselves over whether they should "lean in" to be more aggressive careerists; whether it is okay to even mention a woman's gender when writing about her scientific accomplishments; whether an obituary can discuss the deceased woman's domestic skills (and in which paragraph such information belongs); whether women at Ivy League schools should seize the opportunity to find husbands among their intellectually equal classmates (or whether this is a deeply regressive anti-feminist impulse); and whether a woman CEO is betraying the sisterhood if she outlaws telecommuting.[3]*

---

[3] Gene Weingarten, "Why Is the Feminist Movement in an Identity Crisis? Just Look at the Back of Your Jeans," Washington Post, April 25, 2013, https://www.washingtonpost.com/life-style/magazine/why-is-the-feminist-movement-in-an-identity-crisis-just-look-at-the-back-of-your-jeans/2013/04/24/000d54c2-9e18-11e2-a941-a19bce7af755_story.html?utm_term=.84d26a6a82ff.

If you're reading this, you're most likely a woman, and we're betting that your life is probably very, very complex. Your grandmother and definitely her mother lived in much simpler times. The choices available to them in life were few; women were caretakers: wives and mothers, possibly with short-lived careers as teachers or nurses. Then came the feminist movement, which told us it was time to take charge of our own lives, do what we wanted to do when we wanted to do it. On the surface, it sounded like a good idea; and no one was unhappy when women's wages began to rise, and some of those who had deserved promotions for years finally received them. But those things came at a cost. Suddenly, a woman happy in a traditional role of wife and mother was told she was selling herself short. Why wasn't she out there producing like a man? After years of being told it was her job to raise the next generation and find her identity in doing so, suddenly she was a failure—a disappointment to all other women if that was *all* she did. No, now she was supposed to have a professional life. And yet at the same time, she was still responsible for the needs of her family. Fathers may have done more to "help," but the main responsibility for the family's day-to-day well-being still rested squarely on the woman's shoulders. Somehow, she had to do it all.

"When I think about what I feel is expected of me today as a woman, 'more' is the only word that comes to mind," says Emily, a twenty-one-year-old investment advisor.

"Today, middle-class women have 'more' in the most positive sense of the word—more representation, access to education, and the ability to build a career. We see in our own workplaces what our colleagues who are mothers go through balancing family and career. The emotional labor of being a mother and wife has not changed. My female co-workers are still the first person the school calls when their child is sick at school. They're still the ones expected to plan the birthday parties. They're still the ones ensuring that every member of their family is secure, healthy, and content before themselves. With more women entering the workforce, these expectations have not gone away. Women instead silently accept this reality while taking on the same amount of professional labor as their male peers."

The truth is, no one can do it all, at least not without sacrificing something. If a woman steals time from her family to succeed in business, she is wracked by guilt. If she sacrifices her career for the sake of her family, she may feel like she's not making good use of her talents and helping her husband provide for the family. She can't win either way.

Indra Nooyi is considered one of the world's one hundred most powerful women. As PepsiCo's first female chief executive, she earned an annual salary of nearly $30 million, boosting revenue by eighty percent during her leadership of the company. When she left PepsiCo, however, she remarked, "I've been blessed with an amazing career, but if I'm being honest, there have been moments I wish I'd spent more time with my children." Nooyi told how her daughter once wrote her a letter when she was about four or five years old that said, "Dear mom, please, please, please, please, please come home. I love you, but I'd love you more if you came home." Nooyi said she kept the letter to remind her of what she had lost.

The night that she was promoted to PepsiCo CEO, she left the office in the early evening (rather than working until midnight as she usually did) to go home and share the news with her family. Her mother met her at the door and asked her to go get milk for breakfast the next morning. When she asked her mother why she had not sent their house help for the milk earlier, her mother explained that she had forgotten. Nooyi then asked why her mother hadn't asked Nooyi's husband to get the milk, as he'd been home for several hours. "He was tired," she responded. Nooyi went out for the milk.[4]

In some ways, everything has changed for women. And nothing has. Thirty-five-year-old business manager Brittany says, "We are supposed to have children like we don't work, and work like we don't have children while maintaining an orderly home, preparing organic meals, looking beautiful, volunteering, and maintaining a relationship with our husbands."

Younger women today grew up steeped in the self-esteem movement of the 1990s. Raised to love

[4]Marilyn Haigwwh, "Indra Nooyi Shared a Work Regret on Her Last Day as PepsiCo CEO," Make It CNBC, October 03, 2018, https://www.cnbc.com/2018/10/03/indra-nooyi-shares-a-work-regret-on-her-last-day-as-pepsico-ceo.html.

themselves, they were taught in classroom exercises how special they were, with the theory of the day being that high self-esteem would carry them to success, despite societal pressures pulling them one way and another. When all the balls women are juggling come crashing down today, what remains? Without a sense of identity, worth, and value outside of what we do or don't accomplish, with continued oppression in many parts of the non-Western world, women often face what has been called "the logical despair of womanhood."

Women the globe over are more likely than men to experience psychological distress. Suicide has become the leading worldwide killer of teenage girls ages fifteen to nineteen, confirms founding director of the Centre for Global Mental Health, Vikram Patel: "The most probably [sic] reason is gender discrimination. Young women's lives [in South East Asia] are very different from young men's lives in almost every way." He noted that women in India are often devastated to learn how limited their life choices are because of their gender. "Fifty percent of those attempting suicide in China and India do not have mental illness," he continued. "They suffer logical despair."[5]

When you ask yourself, "Am I a person of value?" if your answer is yes, you have a sense of your self-worth. If you're unsure or if you truly believe you have little value in this world, your life will be a constant struggle. Your inner world will be a roller coaster of thinking you're fine one day and not so fine the next. If we look at our worth from a human perspective, then we will always see something "flawed and weak." We may swing from relatively happy with ourselves to insecurity and, yes, despair. But God's perspective is eternal, and by His power, we *can* do the things He has created each of us to do.

This doesn't mean, however, that we can literally do everything: build a successful career, raise awesome children, be great lovers and friends with smiles on our faces. No, we will always be "made of dust," and our physical frame—not to mention our emotional one—simply can't "do it all." But

[5] Joanna Rothkopf, "The 'Logical Despair' of Womanhood: Women Are Much More Likely to Suffer Psychological Distress Than Men," Salon, May 29, 2015, https://www.salon.com/2015/05/29/the_logical_despair_of_womanhood_women_are_much_more_likely_to_suffer_psychological_distress_than_men/.

when our worth comes from what God says about us, when we are secure in *Him*, we will find we have greater wisdom to discern which things God's Spirit is calling us to do and which things are actually unnecessary. We will be better able to leave our failures in God's hands, knowing that it is His strength, not our own, at work in our lives. He can work all things to His glory, despite our personal weakness.

## EMBRACING THE WORD

*"You are precious and honored in my sight,*
*and. . .I love you."*
ISAIAH 43:4

Dr. W. David Hager, in his book *As Jesus Cared for Women*, voices some of the "hand-wringing" crises of identity we've talked about in this chapter, things that rock our sense of worth as women.

*"Should I follow career or personhood or*
*marriage?" "Should I be strong or coy?". . .*
*"Can I be satisfied in life as a single person?"*
*Because their pace of life is so hectic, many*

*women never pause long enough to make
careful decisions about these matters. Only a
loving heavenly Father can lead them through
the frantic maze and into a place of peace and
grace. It is difficult to hear His voice, however,
when they are burdened by excessive demands
of work, family, and friends. It takes time to
listen to God, but these times of meditation
are important because this is when God can
impress upon the listener that her true worth
and value is found in the intimacy of her
relationship with Him.*[6]

## GOING FURTHER. . .

1. Have you struggled with trying to do it all, to be "enough?"

2. How has the feminist movement helped women? Do you feel that it hurt us?

3. Is there any "white space" in your life, downtime where you can listen to God speak to you personally?

---

[6] W. David Hager, *As Jesus Cared for Women* (Grand Rapids, MI: Fleming H. Revell, 1998), 87.

# CHAPTER 3

$\sim$

# How to Prevent an Identity Crisis

## *Dealing with Life's Changes*

Today, there are more voices than ever before telling you who you should be, what your face, your body, your clothes, your home, your family, and your social life should look like and what you should be accomplishing! The theory of "social comparison" explains how we determine our personal self-worth based on our comparison to others. It's surprising to think it's still considered a "theory" though. Most of us would probably admit that we can't help ourselves—we unconsciously compare ourselves to every beautifully edited and filtered image we scroll through on social media every day. There are few of us who haven't been caught in the comparison trap.

This is the first time in history that a woman has ever even had the opportunity to see never-ending images of other women. Author Beth Moore points out that "most of our great-great-grandmothers had access to compare themselves to a few hundred women in a lifetime."[7] Especially if you're a millennial, you've grown up with social media so that consuming it is as natural as breathing and drinking water! The result? "We no longer feel inferior to ten other women the way our great-grandmothers might have. We feel inferior to thousands and as a result, we become less and less satisfied with ourselves until much of our lives are lived on the slippery slope of self-loathing. . .we are the pathetic few that can't keep up."[8]

Since we're a 24-7 global village now, the pressure is worldwide. Julia Peters, twenty-two, lives in Leicestershire, Great Britain. She says, "There is an unwritten rule about how you should look in your pictures—how you should do your makeup and what filter you should use. A lot of people can't cope with the anxiety if they see someone has criticized a photo or posted a picture that looks better than theirs."[9]

[7] Beth Moore, *So Long, Insecurity, You've Been a Bad Friend to Us* (Carol Stream, IL: Tyndale House Publishers, 2010), 92.

[8] Ibid.

[9] Sarah Marsh and Guardian Readers, "Girls and Social Media: 'You Are Expected to Live Up to an Impossible Standard,'" *The Guardian*, August 22, 2017, https://www.theguardian.com/society/2017/aug/23/girls-and-social-media-you-are-expected-to-live-up-to-an-impossible-standard.

Women, especially young women between the ages of fourteen and twenty-five, are experiencing depression and anxiety on an unprecedented scale. "My anxiety is interfering with my life," is one of the "Six Things Millennials Bring Up in Therapy," along with, "I feel like a fraud."[10] "We don't stand a chance," writes twenty-six-year-old blogger Alexa Tanney. "Who stands a chance against someone who is almost perfect? And isn't that what *everyone* is basically doing online? Creating the perfect versions of themselves?"[11]

On the journey from girlhood to womanhood and as we navigate the different seasons of life, the natural question to be grappled with should be *Who am I?* But instead, we may wonder anxiously and daily: *What is expected of me? How do I present to others?* The very way that we define ourselves as people has shifted. Sadly, this now begins as young as eight or nine years old. (We are cultivating our children's

[10] Brittany Wong, "The 6 Things Millennials Bring Up Most in Therapy," *HuffPost*, September 27, 2018, https://www.huffpost.com/entry/millennial-therapy-issues_n_5a0620f2e4b-01d21c83e84d2.

[11] Alexa Tanney, "Social Comparison Theory: How Our Social Media Habits Make Us Unhappy," *Elite Daily*, May 07, 2019, https://www.elitedaily.com/life/media-affects-self-worth/1055695.

online selves from birth—or even before, in utero. Ninety-two percent of American children have an online presence before the age of two.[12]) Counselor Chrystal Wilson Payne says that girls are "branding themselves on social media, pretending before they have any idea of who they are, bringing on a crisis of identity usually seen in mid-life. Young girls start out in crisis. We've seen a shift in young people engaging in self-harm, with depression and anxiety across all socioeconomic and racial backgrounds."[13]

Yes, anyone can end up in an identity crisis. Periods of uncertainty, confusion, and insecurity come to all of us at one time or another, especially in times of change. When our identity is based on the labels we wear, we are positioned for crisis. I am a student. I am an athlete. I am a mother. I am a wife. I am an employee. All our roles in life are subject to change, and we can lose ourselves in these roles. Mothers get lost in motherhood. Wives get lost in bad marriages or in the pursuit of marriage. We

[12] Nancy Jo Sales, "Social Media and Secret Lives of American Teenage Girls," *Time,* n.d., https://time.com/americangirls/.

[13] Chrystal Wilson Payne, interview with Nicole Steele, Priceless Perspective podcast audio, April 24, 2019, *New York Times Book Review,* podcast audio, April 22, 2007, https://shows.pippa.io/pricelessperspectivepodcast/episodes/ep-03.

can get lost in the pursuit of a career or social relationships.

Yet when you look in the mirror, see yourself in a photo, or lie in bed at night with the lights out, are you comfortable with who you are or do you fall short of your own expectations? Very few people are so secure that they never doubt themselves. We all feel inadequate at times.

Mariem Sherif, an Egyptian blogger, describes her friend in crisis:

> *My best friend was telling me lately how afraid she has been thinking about her life. She was telling me how she doesn't know if she's doing anything that matters or if her career is what she wanted to do or what she was forced to do. She was telling me she's even been thinking about love and how she can't see it that someone might love her one day because she doesn't know what's so special about herself that can make her loved. She doesn't know who she is.[14]*

---

[14] "Read This When You're on the Brink of an Identity Crisis (or Already Deep in One)," *Thought Catalog*, February 07, 2017, https://thoughtcatalog.com/mariem-sherif/2017/02/read-this-when-youre-on-the-brink-of-an-identity-crisis-or-already-deep-in-one/.

What about you, right now?

- Do you feel inadequate most of the time?
- Do you find yourself being a different person in different relationships or in different environments?
- Are you allowing yourself to be mistreated by someone?
- Do you long for more meaning, passion, and purpose?
- Have there been major changes in your life such as a divorce, death, graduation, loss of a job, changes in your physical appearance or abilities?

How vulnerable to an identity crisis are you? Explore these thoughts to assess your vulnerability:

## STEP 1:

Be honest with yourself about what gives you your sense of self-worth. List the things that are good about you, as well as what you view as important parts of who you are. You must be brutally honest here. Write down not what you think the list should include, but what you honestly believe. You might include:

1. Your appearance (not only beauty but what you do with your appearance—grooming, your sense of style, etc.)
2. Your career or mission in life
3. Your role as a single or married person
4. Your role as a mother, if applicable
5. What God says about your value (Be careful here. It's easy to write down some Bible verses without thinking through what has become a reality to you.)
6. What others say about you, including your family (Does verbal affirmation make you feel worthwhile?)
7. Your intelligence
8. Your physical fitness
9. Your personality (the ability to make friends and relate to other people)
10. Your character (Do you like living with yourself?)

11. Your skills (social, artistic, and so on)

12. Your achievements, past and present

_____

_____

_____

_____

_____

_____

Now, what else gives you a sense of self-worth?
Write it all down.

_____

_____

_____

_____

_____

_____

_____

What you have jotted down on your list will tell you:

1. Who you are
2. What you do

# STEP 2:

After you have made your list, ask yourself, "Which of these things can change or will be taken away from me at some point in my life?" Put a mark by each source of identity that may change. Again, be honest with yourself. Right now, your marriage may be a good one, but could that change in the future? (If nothing else, the odds are that your husband will die before you do. Sooner or later, most women are widows.) Right now, your young children are enjoyable and loving, but will they be the same as teens or young adults? Right now, you may like yourself, but will you feel the same when you grow older and must deal with illness or physical limitations?

# STEP 3:

Evaluate your vulnerability. What if your kids don't turn out well, or you become disabled or disfigured, or poor, or you never marry, or you lose your job or you lose your husband, or. . . ? How would you feel about yourself then? (Some of us are very good at this game; we worry a lot.) If most of your sense of self-worth comes from sources that at some point in life can or will be taken from you, you are vulnerable to an identity crisis.

At some point in your life (often at midlife), you will look in the mirror and discover you no longer have the attention-getting appearance you once had. You'll feel like you've become invisible. There will be bags under your eyes, something flabby hanging down under your arms—and those arms don't tighten up with the same amount of effort anymore! Marabel Morgan in *Total Joy* speaks of this realization and offers us comfort.

> *Every woman knows she must someday grow old and lose the bloom of youth. Yet when it begins to happen, she registers shock. Wrinkles appear overnight. She sees the law of gravity pulling on her underarms and chin and everything below the chin. Who would have*

*ever thought it could happen to her?*

*While my girls and I were talking about life one day, I told them, "Your body is actually a shell, a 'house' you wear. The real you which is inside your body will someday leave. So if anything happens to your body, it won't affect the real you. Even if you were in an accident and your arms or legs were cut off, the real you would still be intact inside."*

*To me, that's very comforting. Knowing that God designed my house takes great pressure off me. I am not going to fight His design. Someday we'll be free of these bodies and their diseases and limitations, but for now we're stuck inside. I'll change what I can and accept what I can't.*[15]

Still, if your self-esteem has been based on your appearance, accepting the effects of time on your looks can be a painful lesson.

Then one day your last child will leave home and take a huge chunk of your heart with her. Your

---

[15] Marabel Morgan, *Total Joy* (Old Tappan, NJ: Revell, 1976).

"second act" will begin, and you may struggle to figure out what that's supposed to look like. Eventually, you will get up some morning and find that your joints feel stiff. Your eyesight will begin to fail, and you will need at least two pairs of glasses. Moreover, life may not have turned out like you imagined it would. You may be hit with the realization that you never achieved the goals you set for yourself when you were just starting out. You will never write that book, run that marathon, or open that business you have been saving for. Time is running out on you, and you have lost a lot of chances along the way.

Or a major change will come in your life—a death, a disability, career disappointment, or a broken relationship—that will stop you in your tracks and force you to reevaluate yourself. Make no mistake, some of these things happen to us all. How will you cope? Can you prepare yourself in advance for life's inevitable changes?

Of course, we do need and thrive on the encouragement and praise of people who are close to us. And having supportive relationships does much to contribute to our sense of self-worth. We can't underestimate the value of having a community of women to share this journey with you, to listen, to cry with, and to pray with on a daily basis. God gives us clarity and encouragement through one another if we will both allow others to speak into our lives and do the same for them. So often we think of the story of Ashley, a quiet woman who survived (and eventually left) an abusive marriage to an alcoholic husband because her friend faithfully called her every single morning to pray with her.

But we cannot depend totally on others for our self-worth. Because life often brings drastic changes, each of us needs a solid, unchangeable foundation for feeling worthwhile. Go back to your list of sources of identity. Do you have anything listed there that will never change? How about what God says about your value? Do you know what God has said about you in the Bible? If you do know, do you feel like you own it?

One of the saddest letters we ever received was from a sixty-eight-year-old woman who asked, "How good must I be for God to love me?" Abandoned by her mother at birth and not adopted until she was twelve, this woman had deep emotional scars. She suffered from having grown up believing that acceptance—from other people and from God—is based on our looks, our abilities, and our performance.

At the age of fifteen, she attended a church and for the first time heard the salvation message. She responded and received Jesus Christ as her personal Savior, but her joy was overwhelmed by feelings of unworthiness as she went home and knelt by her bed that night. Instead of rejoicing in her new faith, she wept and asked God to let her die because she knew she could never "stay good enough for God to love me." She closed her sad letter with the question "Does God perform plastic surgery of the heart to erase the trauma of childhood?"

Paul wrote to the Ephesians, "He [God] made us accepted in the Beloved [Christ]" (Ephesians 1:6 NKJV). This means that your acceptance by the Father has nothing to do with your goodness or badness; it totally rests upon what Jesus did. Because God accepts you, you can accept yourself. Because God recognizes you as a person of value and worth, you can recognize yourself as one made in His image, important and worthwhile.

The best way you can protect yourself from a personal crisis is to base your sense of self-worth primarily on the one source that does not change: God. God loves you! John 3:16 says He loves you so much that He gave His only Son for you. Has that truth sunk into your core? Do you really believe that Jesus died for you? It's not hard to believe He died for *us*—collectively—but do you feel He died for *you*—personally? Could He have loved you that much, when He had a whole world of people to deal with? You think you are one unimportant individual, and sometimes it feels as if He doesn't even know you exist. But He does.

It's a hard fact to grasp. I can't understand why He loves me with such an intense love. In our evaluation of ourselves, we're not worth that kind of love. We know our faults very well, and we do not deserve His love. But what we feel about ourselves has nothing to do with the fact that, despite everything, God loves us, He loves you—and always will. There is no greater statement of worth than that!

No matter what you look like, no matter what

you do or don't do, nothing changes the fact that God loves you. The world you live in may say you have little value, but God says you are so valuable to Him that He gave His Son to suffer and be crucified so you—you, the individual—could live with Him forever. That is the bedrock upon which you must build your life and from which you can gain an identity that nothing can destroy.

You are a work of art that God is creating. How much is a piece of art worth? Well, that depends on what someone is willing to pay for it. Obviously, an art collector would pay a lot more for the *Mona Lisa* than for something you doodled as you waited on hold on the phone. How much was God willing to pay for you? An enormous price—the life of His only Son, given through an agonizing death! He didn't do that for any other part of His creation. He did it only for those of us made in His image. Whether you feel like it or not, you are supremely valuable to Him—a *Mona Lisa*, not a scribble or doodle. An exquisite work of craftsmanship and beauty.

Sometimes something that's been overlooked

as a worthless piece of junk turns out to be more valuable than we would ever have dreamed. Richard Rusthton-Clem of Lewisburg, Pennsylvania, bought an old pickle bottle for three dollars at a tag sale. A few months later, he offered it for sale on Ebay, the internet auction site. Much to his surprise, after a week-long auction and more than sixty bids, the eleven-inch amber bottle sold for $44,100! Some mornings do you wake up feeling worth about as much as a three-dollar pickle bottle? Do you feel that about all you're good for is to sit on a shelf? Take heart! You're worth far more than $44,100! God was willing to pay the death of His only Son to redeem you. Not only that, but He has committed Himself to be available at all hours to listen to your prayers. He has promised never to leave you or abandon you. He is preparing a home for you to live with Him forever. You're priceless! Never forget it!

Your heart may tell you something different. So will the world. And most of all, Satan will try to convince you that you're not worth much at all. After all, if you spend all your time being discouraged with yourself, you won't be as available to God for His use. Satan would love to foil God's plan for your life.

Neil Anderson helps people deal with a damaged sense of their own worth. In his book *The Bondage Breaker*, he says,

> *One of the most common attitudes I have discovered in Christians—even among pastors [and] Christian leaders, and their children—is a deep-seated sense of self-deprecation. I've heard them say, "I'm not important, I'm not qualified, I'm no good." I'm amazed at how many Christians are paralyzed in their witness and productivity by thoughts and feelings of inferiority and worthlessness. . . . Satan can do absolutely nothing to alter our position in Christ and our worth to God. But he can render us virtually inoperative if he can deceive us into listening to and believing his insidious lies accusing us of being of little value to God or other people.[16]*

---

[16] Neil T. Anderson, *The Bondage Breaker* (Eugene, OR: Harvest House, 1990), 141.

Don't listen to Satan's lies. God loves you so much, He gave His own Son for you. You are that valuable to Him.

Your part is to believe God's evaluation of you. Trust Him to accomplish His purpose in your life as you do life with Him one day at a time. In a way, it's so simple, yet it is the opposite of the advice you'll get from our culture.

Whom will you believe?

## EMBRACING THE WORD

*I press on to take hold of that for which*
*Christ Jesus took hold of me.*
PHILIPPIANS 3:12

The apostle Paul had plenty of bad things in his past. Before his conversion, he had been a murderer, a Christian killer; he was even there when Stephen, one of the earliest Church leaders, was stoned to death. After his conversion, I'm sure Satan must have tried to keep Paul obsessed with his past, wallowing in shame and regret over all the horrible things he had done. If Satan could have kept Paul living in the past, then Paul would never have gone on to be the great missionary who spread the Good News throughout the world.

Sometimes, though, we may *like* to live in the past, back when we were younger and stronger, when people we loved so much were still with us and needed us, when we felt competent and more in control of our lives. But God doesn't want us to live in the past any more than He wanted Paul to. Paul said, "But one thing I do: Forgetting what is behind and straining toward what is ahead, I press on toward the goal to win the prize for which God has called me" (Philippians 3:13–14). Whether the past was bad or good, God wants us to "press on."

God understands how weak we really are. In Psalm 103:14, we read that "he knows how we are formed, he remembers that we are dust." While challenging us in Matthew 5:48 to be mature or complete—"Be perfect, therefore, as your heavenly Father is perfect"—He provides a way for us when we fall short: confession and forgiveness. "If we confess our sins, he is faithful and just and will forgive us our sins and purify us from all unrighteousness" (1 John 1:9).

Our goal in life should not be to pursue what the world says is valuable but to strive to be what God says is valuable. We should endeavor to take hold not of someone else's reason for being but of God's purpose for us. We do not have to place a price tag on our value. God has already done that. Our job is to "press toward the mark" of God's purpose for us and to leave the rest to Him. Even if we appear to be failures to the world we live in, the Bible says that "he who began a good work in you will carry it on to completion until the day of Christ Jesus" (Philippians 1:6). We can rely on that.

## GOING FURTHER...

1. Why does Satan want you to undervalue yourself?

2. Have you ever experienced an identity crisis? If so, when? What brought it on?

3. An identity crisis is not just for teens or mid-life. It can overtake us whenever our lives change in some way if we have been depending on something other than God for our self-worth. Are there major changes looming

ahead of you in your life? If so, what are they? Do you think they will shake your sense of your own value? Are you at risk for an identity crisis? Why or why not?

4. Identity crises are never pleasant, but they can force us to realize that we have been looking to something other than God for our value. Out of the pain, we can emerge with a stronger faith and a true, biblical sense of our own worth. If you are not currently in a crisis, do you know someone who is? Pray for her today that she will use this painful time as an opportunity to know God and His purpose for her life more deeply.

*Dear Jesus, I believe in You—and I want to find my value only in You. But You know how easy it is for me to get distracted. Before I know it, I'm depending on my talents or my natural abilities, my relationships, and my possessions for my worth. Lord, please remind me again and again that time will change all these things, but You will never change. When my identity is*

*rooted in You, I don't have to fear the future.*
*Thank You that You will love me no*
*matter what. Amen.*

# CHAPTER 4

❧

## A Mistake or a Masterpiece?

### A Woman's Basis for Self-Esteem

"All my life I've struggled with being too tall," Sarah confided. From the day she started school, she was a foot taller than anyone else in her class. At the end of the school day, she would run home crying, trying to escape the taunts of the other children. People stared at her as if she were some kind of freak. When she was thirteen, her parents put her in the hospital for hormone treatments to stop her growth, but they were unsuccessful. To make matters worse, people often compared her to her younger sister, who was of average height and considered prettier than she. Sarah grew up feeling she was a big mistake.

Struggling with a lack of self-esteem, she began to compensate for her tallness in various ways. She got good grades, became proficient in four languages, achieved in athletics, and eventually earned a law degree and began a successful career. But underlying all her achievement was the gnawing feeling that God had messed up when He made her. This feeling affected everything she did.

## BONNIE:

Different—that's how I felt from about the time I was old enough to look in a mirror and then look at everyone else around me. It was. . .the hair! Clearly, hair was supposed to grace the head like smooth silk, flowing down onto the shoulders in perfect order. But what was the stuff sprouting from my head, rebelliously twisting and turning in no order at all, fuzzy and frizzy?

My three-year-old mind thought, *It's my brain waves! Hair is obviously brain waves that grow out of your head, and my brain is different than everyone else's!* Every Saturday night, my poor mother tried rollers, pinning it down, and even taping it to my cheeks, but to no avail. The next morning it would be coiling this way and that, doing its own thing again. I would try to avoid swimming, rush back to my college dorm room to straighten it before dinner, and avoid photos at the beach at all costs. As a teen in the long, straight-hair 1970s, I felt *ugly*.

## DARLENE:

I was born with a dark port wine birthmark on the left side of my face. I learned to get used to people staring and kids asking, "What's that on your face?" I admit this is a very minor thing to be concerned about. Many people have *major* physical issues that draw finger-pointing and unkind comments. Butto me, as a kid, it was major.

Eventually, my mom found a makeup that would help conceal the birthmark. Life was better. But the color was not right for me and made me look as if I had hit the side of my face with a big white powder puff. I then got the comment, "Why do you have powder on your face?" Feeling different from everyone else in any way is debilitating! I just wanted to sink into a hole in the ground.

How about you? Have you struggled with some of these same feelings? Is there an aspect of your physical self that has strongly impacted your sense of worth? Do you have a hard time, like our tall friend, Sarah, did, with your attitude toward God, whom Sarah could not see as a loving, perfect Father. To her, God was not perfect—not when He had made such mistakes when He made her. But here's the thing: The Bible says that you were created by God. It actually says that you were "knit together" in your mother's womb (Psalm 139:13). Every artist likes to choose the frame that best displays his or her work. It is not a mistake that you are tall, have curly hair, a birthmark or any particular personality type. If God had wanted you to be five feet, five inches tall, with a head of glossy straight hair and flawless skin, He would have made you that way. You are not a mistake. You are exactly the perfect canvas on which He wants to display His beauty—inside and out, and your body is the frame for the Artist's work.

This is certain: you can be what God created you to be. The apostle Paul wrote, in Philippians 3:12 (NKJV), "Not that I have already attained, or am already perfected; but I press on, that I may lay hold of that for which Christ Jesus has also laid hold of me." Let's break that down:

1. Christ Jesus has laid hold of me for a purpose.

2. I am not yet all I can be.

3. My goal is to lay hold of that purpose for which Jesus laid hold of me.

The freeing part of that truth is that God doesn't expect you to be anything you don't have the capability to be. God's purpose for you and His expectations of you are in line with your gifting. You don't have to fulfill anyone else's purpose for being—only what God has designed you to fulfill. You don't have to be envious of anyone else's abilities and accomplishments because His purpose for you is unlike His plan for another. You can admire what is admirable in another's life and ask God to make that a reality in your life. But that's up to the Holy Spirit to accomplish; it's not something we need to strive for on our own. Simply do the things He made you good at doing and see how He will use you to fulfill His will. If you do, you will experience the highest sense of fulfillment you can have in your life. Then you can say, "I'm doing what God designed me to do. I'm laying hold of my purpose for being on this earth." And you will have joy.

But perhaps you struggle with depression, anxiety, or other physiological trauma or have a disability. Or maybe your outlook on life has been warped by parents who constantly told you that you were no good, that you would never amount to anything in life—and you still believe them. Possibly you've done something that you feel has disqualified you for a life of value and purpose, and you have never forgiven yourself. Perhaps you are a victim of rape, sexual molestation, incest, or some other set of horrible circumstances that you had no control over but still feel guilty about. Whatever happened to you in the past, the end result is that you don't think very highly of yourself. You have given up trying to be all that you could be. *What's the use?* you think. Perhaps you have also given up on God, believing that somewhere in your life, either you or He messed up on the master plan.

It may be that the very thing you hate most about yourself is actually the canvas God will use for the beautiful work of art He plans to create out of your life. Accepting a concept like this means you must look at yourself in an entirely new way—and that won't be easy, particularly if you've been hating something about yourself for years, maybe even for your entire life. But try to shift your perspective until you can look at yourself from God's viewpoint. You might be surprised by what you see.

We can't say, however, that every bad thing that has happened to you has been God's will for your life. Some things have come about through the actions of others or the actions of nature, so blaming God for every bad thing in your life is unfair. He has given us free will and great latitude in our actions, and there are people in the world who take advantage of their free will to hurt the lives of others. For now, we can't give a reason for the effect of sin and evil in this world—and in your life and mine—apart from the fact that Satan has been given limited domain in this world for a period of time. There is a set time for the end of evil. But men and women, starting with Adam and Eve, have yielded to his temptations with the result that, until Christ returns and destroys Satan, we will struggle with both the power and the effects of sin in this world.

you understand just who you truly are, you'll have a clearer idea of what God's perspective on your life really is. That's what we're going to do in the next chapter.

## EMBRACING THE WORD

*I was given a thorn in my flesh, a messenger of Satan, to torment me. Three times I pleaded with the Lord to take it away from me. But he said to me, "My grace is sufficient for you, for my power is made perfect in weakness." Therefore I will boast all the more gladly about my weaknesses, so that Christ's power may rest on me. . . . For when I am weak, then I am strong.*
2 CORINTHIANS 12:7–10

Just think—even Paul the apostle had something about himself that hurt him, something that he wished God would just take away. We don't know what that thing was, although Bible experts have had all sorts of theories. It might have been an illness or some sort of physical disability; it may even have been a personality problem; but whatever it was, Paul felt it made him less than perfect. And he asked God to take what he called his "thorn in the flesh" away from him.

What are the "thorns" that torment you? Almost everyone has one of one sort or another. Yours may not be an issue of your appearance. Maybe you are dyslexic or you don't fluently speak the language that is used where you live. Maybe you don't *ever* want anyone to know about the addiction, abuse in your family, or about your uncle who is in prison for murder. Each person's "thorn" is different; but whatever it is, it acts as a messenger from Satan. It whispers to us, "You're not good enough. A person with *this* problem will never accomplish much of anything. You just don't measure up."

Satan certainly can use that thorn to torment us. But guess what? God can use it too, in an entirely different way. He will use that ugly, painful thorn to bring Him glory and show you grace.

That's why when Paul prayed that his personal "thorn in the flesh" be taken away, God told him "No" three times until Paul finally got the message. At last Paul understood that the very thing that hurt him so much, the thing that Satan had been using to speak his lies, that same awful thing was the very opportunity that Christ needed to show His power and grace in Paul's life.

If we could do everything perfectly, eventually we'd get pretty arrogant. If we thought nothing about us could be improved, we wouldn't think we needed God at all; we'd assume we could do everything in our own strength without any help from Him. That's why Paul says that when he is weak, he is strong. The very thing that reminds us of our own imperfection can also be the thing that turns us to God. And whenever we acknowledge our own weakness, God has the chance, yes, He longs, to pour out His strength in our lives.

The secret is to refuse to listen to Satan's lies. Instead, turn to God immediately whenever your "thorn" jabs you. Despite your weakness—no, *because* of your weakness—Christ's power can be your strength.

*P.S. Sarah now wears high heels, Bonnie rocks her curls and with laser surgery and a bit of concealer, Darlene glows!*

## GOING FURTHER. . .

1. Have you ever felt that God made a mistake in the way He made you? Have you felt He made a mistake when He allowed some circumstance to happen in your life? Are you still angry at God about this?

2. Can you think of ways that God has already or may yet turn that "mistake" into a blessing? Look at your life prayerfully and write them down. Whenever you get discouraged with yourself, read the list to remind yourself that God is working in your life.

3. Is there something in your life that you still can't see as a potential blessing? Write it down, and then pray every day that God will show you a way that He can use this "mistake" to His glory and your blessing. He *will* answer your prayer; and when He does, make sure you write down whatever new insight He has shown you. (Satan will be all too ready to make your "blessing" look like a "mistake" again, so it's good to have a written record.)

4. Write Psalm 139:14 on a note card, and put it over your bathroom sink or some other place where you will see it often.

*Dear God, You know the thing I like least about myself. You know how long I have struggled with feelings of insecurity and self-doubt because of this thing. I'm not sure I can bring myself yet to thank You for making me this way, not when I hate this thing so much. But Father, I know You don't make mistakes. And I know You were there when I was being created inside my mother's womb, and You've been there every day since then. And I know You love me. So, dear God, I put myself in Your hands—all of me, even this thing about myself that I don't like very much. Please use me to Your glory. Use even this thing that I hate. Maybe someday I'll be able to see Your plan. And in the meantime, I'll trust You. Go ahead, God—create a work of art in my life. Amen.*

# CHAPTER 5

※

## Who, Where, Why?

### Women and Life's Basic Questions

It's time to turn to the four great questions of life because you'll never know who you are, or Whose you are, without finding answers to them:

*Who am I?*
*Where did I come from?*
*Why am I here?*
*Where am I going?*

The answers you accept to these questions are everything.

Maybe you feel that you've found the answer to one or two. If you google them, you'll have a very long rabbit hole to go down. Philosophy and theology hold out answers, but we really need to know what God says about these four gigantic issues. If we don't know who we are, where we came from, why we are here, and where we are going, how can we ever know and accept our real selves or even begin to live the lives God wants us to live?

Let's see what the Bible says about these questions, one by one.

## WHO AM I?

*1. You are a completely unique individual.*

Among all the other 3.7 billion women in the world, there is no one exactly like you. No one else sees with your eyes, hears with your ears, thinks your thoughts, or feels what you feel. You are one of a kind. Regardless of how you were conceived— whether you were an "accident" or the gift of life cherished and longed for by the two people who gave you life—you were created by God's will. It was God who deigned to give you life when 200,000 sperm competed with one another to fertilize the ovum and made you who you are. Just think of this: If another sperm had won the race, you would not be you! You would be a sister to yourself, similar in some ways to who you are now but also uniquely different. Have no doubt about it, you were meant to be born, and you were meant to be exactly who you are. Your identity is the result of neither coincidence nor accident. You are who you are because of God's loving design. He wanted you to be exactly *you* and no one else.

## 2. You were created in the image of God.

How do you respond to that statement? Do you believe it with your head but not with your heart? All of your sins and flaws and failures whisper to you, *"You're* not much like God." If you listen, you'll be overwhelmed with discouragement and self-hatred. Your heart will feel too dark to ever contain the brilliance of God's image.

Are you willing, despite your feelings of inadequacy and inferiority, to accept what God says about you? Stop and think about the power of the verse that says you were created "in the image of God." Because you are created in His image, you have the power to think, to reason, to converse, and to live forever. Unlike animals, for example, you can express yourself in ways that come only through the touch of the divine on your life. We are creators, made to create, because we are miniatures of a Creator.

At creation, God made Adam from the dust of the ground. Then He took a rib from Adam to make Eve. Notice that Adam wasn't the only one made in God's image. So was Eve. Genesis 1:27 tells us, "So God created mankind in his own image. . .male and female he created them." It follows, then, that. . .

*3. You are a woman descended from Eve, who was created from Adam's rib by the hand of God and therefore doubly refined at creation.*

The story goes that after God made Adam, He looked him over and said, "I can do better than that!" and He made a woman! But seriously, the Bible says that after God made Adam from the dust of the ground, He took one of Adam's ribs and, according to the literal rendering of the Hebrew text, "built He a woman." Woman was God's final creative act, the crown of creation!

This double refinement resulted in remarkable differences between men and women. Researchers say that new technologies have generated a "growing pile of evidence that there are inherent differences in how men's and women's brains are wired and how they work."

Women excel in several measures of verbal ability—pretty much all of them, except for verbal analogies. Women's reading comprehension and writing ability consistently exceed that of men on average. They outperform men in tests of fine-motor coordination and perceptual speed. They're more adept at retrieving information from long-term memory.

Men, on average, can more easily juggle items in working memory. They have superior visuospatial skills: They're better at visualizing what happens when a complicated two- or three-dimensional shape is rotated in space, at correctly determining angles from the horizontal, at tracking moving objects, and at aiming projectiles.

Many of these cognitive differences appear quite early in life. You see sex differences in spatial-visualization ability in two- and three-month-old infants. . . infant girls respond more readily to faces and begin talking earlier. Boys react earlier in infancy to experimentally induced perceptual discrepancies in their visual environment. In adulthood, women remain more oriented to faces, men to things.[17]

But being different has nothing to do with being superior or inferior. Sexual differences are all part of God's design and purpose for our lives, something many cultures (and many men) have never grasped. The ancient rabbis, who thanked God that they were neither Gentiles nor women, just didn't get it. When it comes to being a person of value, no one sex has the advantage. Both patriarchy and matriarchy fail to show a complete picture of God's will.

*4. You are a sinner.*

---

[17] Bruce Goldman and Gerard DuBois, "How Men's and Women's Brains Are Different," *Stanford Medicine* (Spring 2017). https://stanmed.stanford.edu/2017spring/how-mens-and-womens-brains-are-different.html.

This is not gender specific; it is true of us all. The Bible says simply, "All of us, like sheep, have strayed away. We have left God's paths to follow our own. Yet the LORD laid on him the sins of us all" (Isaiah 53:6 NLT). Because I am a woman, I am no more a saint than a man nor less a sinner. "All have sinned," is Paul's declaration in Romans 3:23. Sin is an equal opportunity failing.

*5. Because of God's love in Christ Jesus, if you have put your trust in Him, you are a new person, God's child. This means:*

You are adopted into God's family; you are the daughter of the King. This is not just a poetic phrase. It's a fact. Every mother loves her child, but an infant who is adopted is doubly loved because of a decision—a conscious act of the will—to be a mother to that particular child. This is what God says He has done for us.

"Why is God punishing my baby for what I did?" a young mother asked, with scalding tears pouring down her cheeks. Her baby was lying in a crib, a tiny little girl not expected to live beyond the age of two because she had been born with five holes in her heart.

Was God punishing this child for the sexual past of her mother, before she heard the message of Jesus and became a believer? No, not if you believe what the Bible says about forgiveness. God said, "I, yes, I alone am he who blots away your sins for my own sake and will never think of them again" (Isaiah 43:25 TLB). When God forgives, He wipes the slate clean as though you had never sinned. He certainly does not punish your children for sins you committed, sins He forgave you for as soon as you asked His forgiveness.

(We prayed that God would heal the holes in the tiny heart of that infant so her mother would know that when God forgives, He forgets our sins. The last time we had contact with them, the little baby was a young adult. . .in excellent health.)

## WHERE DID I COME FROM?

Psalm 139:13, 15–16 tells us that each of us is individually formed: "You created my inmost being;

you knit me together in my mother's womb. . . . My frame was not hidden from you when I was made in the secret place, when I was woven together. . . Your eyes saw my unformed body; all the days ordained for me were written in your book before one of them came to be."

How do these truths, which we really may not be able to fully understand, give us value? Let's put these facts together and see what they imply. First, God created us in His image. A creator puts something of herself into anything she makes; part of God is in each of us because we are something He made.

Since God put all the parts of you together exactly as He did, it means that He has a purpose for you as you are. You may wish that He had made you more like someone else. You may feel that if you were more like someone else, you would be of more value. But if God had wanted someone like that person, He would have created you that way. You are the person you are because God wanted someone just like you.

As Rick Warren[18] puts it, you have a God-given

---

[18] Rick Warren, *The Purpose-Driven Church* (Grand Rapids, MI: Zondervan, 1996).

SHAPE unlike that of any other person:

> S—spiritual gifts (Read 1 Corinthians 12 and
>    Romans 12)
> H—heart desires
> A—abilities
> P—personality
> E—life experiences

You may never in your entire lifetime understand why you are like you are, but God created you to be His hands and feet in the here and now. *He created you for a purpose*—and that makes you a person of value.

But you are not merely an unduplicated snowflake of God's creation, special simply because you are unique. No, you are far more valuable than that because God loves you. In fact, He loves you so much that, at great personal cost, He did what was necessary so that you could have relationship with Him: He sent His only Son, Jesus Christ, to earth to die by crucifixion on a cross to pay the price that you deserved to pay for your sins—death.

Are you worth the price God paid for you? You

may not think so, but He does. God's desire for relationship with you is so great that He did the unthinkable: He put His holy, beloved Son through the agony of crucifixion. If you ever doubt that you are valuable, read John 3:16 again and remind yourself of the price He paid for you: "For God so loved the world that he gave his one and only Son, that whoever believes in him shall not perish but have eternal life."

## WHY AM I HERE?

When you look to God and what He says in the Bible about your reason for being alive, it takes the spotlight off you and puts it on Jesus. Scripture is clear about this. "He died for all, that those who live should no longer live for themselves but for him who died for them" (2 Corinthians 5:15). My job is to learn what God wants me to do for Him. One of those jobs is to bring God glory: "You [God] created all things, and by your will they were created" (Revelation 4:11). We know that we were created to bring glory to God, because He says of those who are called by His name "whom I created for my glory" (Isaiah 43:7). We bring Him glory when we represent Him well here and now.

You are here to reflect God's beauty, and when we say beauty, we're not just talking about your physical form. Eve was God's final masterpiece of creation. She was the last thing God made, and in woman, God chose to reveal beauty. Yes, God is truth. Yes, God is goodness. But beauty is essential to His very nature. God Himself is described in terms of radiant beauty in the last book of the Bible.

> *The one sitting on the throne was as brilliant as gemstones—like jasper and carnelian. And the glow of an emerald circled his throne like a rainbow. . . . In front of the throne was a shiny sea of glass, sparkling like crystal (Revelation 4:3, 6 NLT).*

Beauty also speaks rest and peace to us. Have you been in a beautiful place—maybe a garden or on an empty beach? In such a place, "There is room for your soul. It expands. You can breathe again. You can rest."[19]

---

[19] John Eldredge and Stasi Eldredge, *Captivating: Unveiling the Mystery of a Woman's Soul* (Nashville, TN: Thomas Nelson, 2010), 39.

Beauty nourishes, comforts, and inspires. And it is transcendent. It is "our most immediate experience of the eternal."[20] When was the last time you really paused to take something in because it was so wonderful? The way an apricot tastes just off the tree? Reading something that captured your thoughts better than you knew possible? A smell or color that was completely new? What moment has made you feel outside of yourself? What experience did you hope would go on forever? Sometimes the beauty is so deep, it pierces us with longing. For what? For life as it was meant to be. "Beauty says, There is a glory calling to you. And if there is a glory, there is a source of glory."[21]

Do you struggle with knowing God's will for your life? Whatever your career, your role as a mother, wife or friend, you bring beauty to the world!

So too psychology confirms that you have a heart for relationship that is reflective of the nature of God. We are more social and relational in the

<hr />

[20] Ibid, 41.

[21] Ibid.

way we think. We naturally think and internalize the feelings of others and react to them.[22] "This vast desire and capacity that a woman has for intimate relationships tells us of God's vast desire and capacity for intimate relationships. In fact, this may be the most important thing we ever learn about God—that He yearns for relationship with us."[23]

*But Zion said, "The LORD has forsaken me, the Lord has forgotten me." "Can a mother forget the baby at her breast and have no compassion on the child she has borne? Though she may forget, I will not forget you!" (Isaiah 49:14–15, 18)*

*I will give them a heart to know me, that I am the LORD. They will be my people, and I will be their God, for they will return to me with all their heart (Jeremiah 24:7).*

---

[22] Gregg Henriques, "The Relational Styles of Men and Women," Psychology Today, September 11, 2013, https://www.psychologytoday.com/us/blog/theory-knowledge/201309/the-relational-styles-men-and-women.

[23] Eldredge, 29.

*"Jerusalem, Jerusalem. . .how often I have longed to gather your children together, as a hen gathers her chicks under her wings, and you were not willing" (Matthew 23:37).*

As women, we reflect God's relational nature as we are usually the relationship cultivators in our families, workplaces, and communities. Eric calls his wife, Elizabeth, "the Queen of Connections," as she is always thinking of who should be introduced to whom, who should know about that job opening, and who she needs to get together with since it's been a while.

Given our personal talents and abilities, we must decide what we are to do with our lives. Whatever choices we make, the point is that our passions, abilities, and gifts are keys to serving God with our lives, in "putting Him and His Kingdom first." A barista can do that just as well as a chair of the board of directors.

In *Hugs for Women*, Mary Hollingsworth speaks of our unique roles in God's kingdom.

> *God needs you too. Whatever gifts and abili-*
> *ties He gave you, He needs you to be at work*
> *in His world and His kingdom. No one else*
> *can do what He designed you for in the same*
> *way you can.*
>
> *No one else can play your role. No one else*
> *knows your lines. You are uniquely created to*
> *fit in the special you-shaped space God formed*
> *in His world.*[24]

Yes, you are the only person born at this precise moment in eternity, in your unique set of circumstances. Here are a few things to ponder as you seek to identify the purpose God created you for:

1. What am I absolutely passionate about? I light up when talking about it!
2. What comes easily for me, so easily that I am quick to discount it as being special?
3. What would I do even if I never got paid for it?
4. When you pray about your purpose, do you

[24] Mary Hollingsworth, *Hugs for Women* (West Monroe, LA: Howard, 1998).

sense God impressing you to go in a certain direction?

5. If what you have to do in this season of your life doesn't "light you up" or is really difficult for you, can you see how you are building something (or investing in someone) that is valuable beyond the here and now?

We love the true story of the woman who loved God and wanted to be a missionary. She longed to share the message of Jesus in places where He was totally unknown. She prepared to go, but in the middle of her training, her sister unexpectedly died, leaving behind three orphaned children. Disappointed, she set aside her dreams and plans and took the children into her care and raised them. She never did achieve her dream of being a missionary. But was her life wasted? No! To her surprise and delight, all three of the children grew up to be missionaries. Her life was actually multiplied because she was faithful to the work God gave her to do, the purpose He created her for!

Yes, prepare for what you think God wants you to do in the future. But live fully today where you are. Today is the day He's given you, and it's the only day you have.

## WHERE AM I GOING?

If you don't live in personal relationship with God, this last question is the scariest because you're not sure if after you die you will spend eternity in heaven or eternally separate from God. But it's the most wonderful to one who is a Christ-follower. When life is over, if you have a personal relationship with Jesus, you are going to be with God. Think of the wonder of these phrases: "I [Jesus] will come back and take you to be with me that you also may be where I am" (John 14:3); "We will be with the Lord forever" (1 Thessalonians 4:17); "at home with the Lord" (2 Corinthians 5:8).

Because Christ gave Himself for us, the very least we can do for Him is to offer our lives in gratitude and surrender. The problem comes when we say, "How could God possibly use my life? Oh yes, He uses missionaries and celebrities. But me? I'm just an ordinary person. I can't do much for God."

Notice that God doesn't ask us to bring just our talents and abilities and all the "good" things in our lives to Him. He asks us to bring everything in our lives—every part of us—and offer ourselves as a living sacrifice for Him to use as He directs (Romans 12:1–2). Some days we may feel proud of what we have to offer God; but other days, maybe most of our days, we'll feel pretty embarrassed about what we have to give Him. He loves us greatly every single day; our actions don't change that. He just wants us to offer ourselves, our wills, and our plans to Him.

Do you have a nasty temper? Give it to God. Do you find discussing other people's business irresistible? Give control of your tongue to God. Are you abusing your body with food? Offer your body to God as a living sacrifice. Let's repeat it: God doesn't want just the "good things." He wants it all. And when we give it to Him, He will use it all, strengths and weaknesses, for His kingdom. Our part is to trust that He is doing just that, whether we can see the results or not.

How can we know how we have affected others in our lifetime? One act of kindness may change another person's life. Your children may seem average and unremarkable to you but have potential as servant leaders, hopefully through your own examples. People might be watching your relationship with your spouse, learning how to resolve conflict with grace and humility, or they may be noting traits that could be important in selecting a future partner. Maybe your kids are grown, and your mentorship could bring hope to a teen struggling with despair or loneliness.

If you have surrendered your life to Jesus, someday you are going to be with Jesus forever and ever. Only then, in heaven, will we know the unseen ways in which God has used us to work in the lives of those around us to accomplish His purposes. Trust Him to use your life—all of it—as a tool of value in His eternal design.

## EMBRACING THE WORD

*But when the set time had fully come, God sent his Son. . .to redeem those under the law, that we might receive adoption to sonship. Because you are his sons,*

*God sent the Spirit of his Son into our hearts, the Spirit who calls out, "Abba, Father." So you are no longer a slave, but God's child; and since you are his child, God has made you also an heir.*
GALATIANS 4:4–7

*The Message* puts Galatians 4:7 like this: "Doesn't that privilege of intimate conversation with God make it plain that you are not a slave, but a child? And if you are a child, you're also an heir, with complete access to the inheritance." The word the apostle Paul used in describing this adoption into the family of God was a legal term. According to Roman law, a person who was adopted could never be prosecuted for former crimes. She received a new name and literally became a new person. So, what does that mean if you are God's adopted child? Well, for one thing, it means you are completely forgiven. You have an entire new identity as God's child. All your old sins belong to the old you, and that person no longer exists. You are a new person in Christ Jesus.

Notice what verse 6 says: "God sent the Spirit of his Son into our hearts." If you grasp that fact, your identity will be radically changed forever. When you give your life to Jesus, He Himself will live inside you. He will be a part of your very heart. And His voice within you will call out to God.

The word *Abba* was the Aramaic word for *Daddy,* a familiar, loving word for a kind and dedicated father. God is the perfect father, including in every way that our earthly fathers fall short. When Jesus lives within you, you have the right to call God, "Daddy," because you are now His beloved child.

## GOING FURTHER...

1. Write a few phrases next to the SHAPE acrostic that describe yourself and make you who you are:

   S-spiritual gifts (Read 1 Corinthians 12 and Romans 12)

   H-heart desires

   A-abilities

   P-personality

   E-life experiences

2. Now, can you prayerfully give each of these things to God? Is there anything that's difficult for you to let go? Why?

3. If you had to sum up your answer in one sentence, why do you think God put you on this earth? For help, see these promises for guidance:

   Proverbs 3:5, 6

   John 8:12

   Isaiah 48:17

   Philippians 1:6

   Psalm 57:2

   Psalm 138:8

4. Do you know for certain where you are going when you die? If not, skip to chapter nine right now and settle that issue with God. Then write a sentence or two about your assurance of eternal life.

Whenever you catch yourself feeling discouraged, whenever you feel as though you just can't "measure up," say to yourself, *Jesus lives in my heart and I am God's child.*

*Jesus, thank You that You hold the answer to all the most important questions in my life. You know who I am, You know where I came from, You know why You put me here, and You know where I am going. Please work through me to accomplish your plan. I give You all of myself. Because of You, Lord, I know I am an entirely new person. Thank You for living in my heart. Thank You that I can call God, "Daddy." Amen.*

# CHAPTER 6

❧

## The Jesus Way to Love Yourself

### Self-Worth, Self-Love, Self-Care

*Visit a farmers' market.*
*Buy a new candle.*
*Go to bed one hour early, and write down*
*   three things you love about yourself.*
*Try a face mask. and go all day without*
*   social media.*
*Take a quick nap.*

We're all pretty stressed these days, no matter what generation we belong to. Caring for ourselves in our world of nonstop global anxiety has us searching for ways to soothe ourselves. If you're a young woman, you may feel the anxiety even more keenly as you struggle to begin your life with a whole lot of uncertainty hanging over your head.

There are *many* ways to help you relax and

nurture yourself, eat healthy, practice good skincare, and stay fit. Internationally, self-care was a $4.2 trillion business in 2017.[25] But besides caring for yourself, the message is everywhere: you must love yourself! Google *self-love* and in less than one second you will have 2.9 billion results to surf through. Scrolling through Instagram, you'll read things like:

> *If you want to create change, self-love is the perfect place to start! Everything changes when you begin to love yourself. You no longer send out energy of desperation or need to be filled from the outside. You become a powerful source within yourself that attracts better. The more you love who you are, the less you seek validation and approval.*[26]

Not that many of us, however, love who we *really* are. If the truth were told, most of us are well aware of our faults. We long to be the very best versions

---

[25] Elaine Low, *"These Self-Care Trends Offer the Ultimate Superfood: Cold, Hard Cash,"* Investors, November 27, 2017, https://www.investors.com/news/self-care-wellness-trends-beauty-fitness-cannabis-market/.

[26] healthyisthenewskinny. "If you want to create change, self-love is the perfect place to start!" Instagram, June 24, 2019, https://www.instagram.com/p/BzGTuJjpRhe/.

of ourselves—to know that we are accomplishing the purpose for which we were created. We do care about others and want to have healthy relationships with them. If you're a follower of Jesus, Bible verses like "Do to others as you would have them do to you" (Luke 6:31); "In humility value others above yourselves" (Philippians 2:3); and Jesus' own words, "Whoever wants to be first must be slave of all" (Mark 10:44), may come to mind as you think about loving yourself and loving others. The Christian life is the way of laying down our lives as Jesus did. So how do we live out the purpose that Jesus created us for and have healthy attitudes toward ourselves?

First, knowing your worth is not the same as loving yourself. Self-love turns inward, away from others. A woman with a true sense of self-worth, however, turns outward to others. When Jesus said, "Love your neighbor as yourself," (Mark 12:31) He knew how much we care for ourselves, and He was telling us we must feel just as much love for those around us as we do for ourselves. A woman who has found a biblical perspective on self-worth is secure enough to serve others, to care for them as much as she cares for herself. She is not selfish, focused on her own self and her own life.

Does that mean we should hate ourselves? Didn't Jesus say, "If anyone comes to me and does not hate. . .even their own life—such a person cannot be my disciple" (Luke 14:26)? Well, we need to understand the context of Jesus' words so we can comprehend what He was really saying. When Jesus made that statement, He was using a form of comparison that was very common in His day. What He is saying is that the love we have for God is to be so great that any other love seems like hatred in comparison. But how could it possibly be right for me to hate myself if God considered me valuable enough to give His Son so I can spend eternity with Him? If God loves me that much, if I am that precious to Him, how can I possibly hate myself?

John R. W. Stott answered the question "Am I supposed to love myself or hate myself?" He says, "[A] satisfactory answer cannot be given *without reference to the Cross*" (italics added). He adds, "The cross of Christ supplies the answer, for it calls us both to self-denial and to self-affirmation" (which he points out is not the same as self-love). Says Stott, "It is only when we look at the cross that we see the true worth of human beings."[27]

If you don't remember any other sentence in this book, we hope you will remember that last one. It is the cross that reveals our true value—your true value. You will find mention of the cross of Jesus and His sacrifice for us many times in this book because the cross turns all that is negative in our lives into something positive. The cross shows us how bad our sins are and does away with them. The cross—in an astounding, mind-boggling way—shows our true worth as God sees it. Only when we understand the price God was willing to pay to forgive us can we feel right about ourselves and experience healthy, biblical self-acceptance.

Yes, Jesus said in Matthew 16:25 (PHILLIPS): "If anyone wants to follow in my footsteps he must give up all right to himself, take up his cross and follow me." In this verse are three conditions to being a true disciple of Christ: (1) give up all right to

[27] John R. W. Stott, "Am I Supposed to Love Myself or Hate Myself?" Christianity Today 20 (April 1984): 26.

oneself; (2) take up a cross; and (3) follow our Lord.

Writer Elisabeth Elliott asks a disconcerting question about this verse: "Can we manage to juggle the building of a stronger self-image while we fulfill those three conditions of discipleship?"[28]

If anyone else had written that last sentence, we might have passed over the words. But this was written by a woman whose husband, along with four other men, was killed at the hands of a tribe in Ecuador while he was trying to reach them with the Gospel. Moreover, Elisabeth was left with a young daughter to raise. Not only was she not bitter, she continued working to reach these people with the message of Jesus and eventually saw many of them become believers. Life grew from seed that had died, producing real and living fruit. If you ever get a chance to see it, it's hard to forget the photograph of her young daughter, Valerie, flying in a missionary airplane on the lap of one of the men—now a believer—who murdered her father. Elisabeth Elliot knew what it means to obey Jesus' call to discipleship!

[28] Elisabeth Elliot, Keep a Quiet Heart (Ann Arbor, MI: Servant, 1995), 195.

So, let's be clear: Self-denial, the sort of self-denial that Christ lived, means that we are to deny all that is selfish in our lives. It does not mean that we go without proper food, rest, exercise, or time alone. We are expected to take care of ourselves! It is not selfish; in fact, it's a way of loving others! Have you heard the story of the Cobbler's Boots?

*Once upon a time, there was a cobbler who was very busy. He lived in a large village and was the only cobbler in town, so he was responsible for repairing the boots of everybody else. However, he didn't have time to repair his own boots. This wasn't a problem at first, but over time, his boots began to deteriorate and fall apart. While he worked feverishly on the boots of everyone else, his feet got blisters and he started to limp. His customers started to worry about him, but he reassured them that everything was OK. However, after a few years, the cobbler's feet were so injured that he could no longer work and no one's boots got repaired. As a consequence, soon*

*the entire town started to limp in pain, all*
*because the cobbler never took the time to*
*repair his own boots.*[29]

The woman who denies herself the things in life that she truly needs to function in a strong and healthy way is really selfishly keeping herself from being at her best for God, her family, and those around her. She is being self-destructive, not spiritual.

Good self-care is personal to each one of us. "Self-care to me looks like learning to listen to very subtle cues. Learning to sense that I'm feeling unwell physically or emotionally and then not ignoring that," says Hannah. "It's giving myself permission to be alone or lie down for a bit to collect myself. I allow myself a fair amount of 'downtime' on my phone or just sitting around and not feeling guilty about resting or doing stuff I enjoy that serves no practical purpose other than to relax or inspire." For Amber, "Self-care to me looks like staying fit, taking care of my body inwardly and outwardly through

---

[29] Darren Poke, "The Cobbler's Boots—A Story About Self-Care." Better Life Coaching Blog, September 29, 2011, https://betterlifecoachingblog.com/2011/08/19/the-cobblers-boots-a-story-about-self-care/.

eating right, exercising, praying, meditating, getting a facial or massage once in a while to treat myself." And self-care will look different during the different seasons of a woman's life; says one retiree, "I take a nap because I can now!"

*Self-denial* has to do primarily with the will. It is a willingness to say yes to anything Jesus wants to do in our lives and to do what He asks of us to the best of our ability, even if we have made other plans. We need to submit our lives to God's leading, to be willing to acknowledge that He has the right to direct the course of our lives. That's not easy. Paul says we are to offer ourselves as "living sacrifice[s]" to God (Romans 12:1). But as someone else said, the problem with living sacrifices is that they keep crawling off the altar!

The thing that is required is to take our eyes off ourselves and put them on Jesus. If we are always looking inward, either to defend ourselves or to see if we're really denying ourselves, we get nowhere.

Remember that Jesus gave us three steps to follow, not just one: deny yourself, take up your cross, and follow Me. When Jesus called His twelve disciples, He called them to follow Him. He didn't organize a committee meeting and draw up a contract for them to sign that outlined the job description and benefits package. He simply said, "Follow Me." What this involves is keeping my eyes on Him, walking where He leads, and obeying Him moment by moment.

It's true, we have no idea where that will lead. Yet it isn't important for us to know the destination or even the path that we will be taking to get there; the One we're following knows the way. Our responsibility is simply to follow. That is the faith that is required to follow Jesus.

The focus of our lives, then, is on God and others rather than on ourselves. Remember that in the two great commandments, Jesus said we are to love God with all our heart, soul, strength, and might, and we are to love our neighbor as ourselves. That's a vertical relationship and a horizontal one. What a contrast to our *self*-centered culture!

If we obey and follow God, will it cost us? Yes. Carrying a cross always costs. As Dietrich Bonhoeffer put it, "When Christ calls a man, he bids him come and die." But have you seen from experience that God is a good Father and you can trust Him with all that is precious to you? Have you found that the greatest satisfaction in life comes when we are living surrendered and pressed into Jesus?

You see, the self-denial Christ calls for is a self-denial with purpose, a self-denial that comes from love—love of God and love of others. Instead of focusing on ourselves, we are free to reach out to others. This is where Philippians 2:3–4 (NLT) comes in: "Don't be selfish; don't try to impress others. Be humble, thinking of others as better than yourselves. Don't look out only for your own interests, but take an interest in others, too." When we focus on God and others, we become relationship-centered. We are free to love, enjoy, and nurture those around us. We are free to meet their needs because we are secure in who we are!

From the book of Romans to the letters of John, the New Testament is full of the phrase "one another." We are told to love one another, honor one another, serve one another, carry each other's burdens, be patient with one another, submit to one another, forgive one another, encourage one another, spur one another on toward love and good deeds, and offer hospitality to one another. The woman who understands her value in God's sight is set free from the need to constantly push herself forward, and she can feel free to reach out to others. As the Holy Spirit works in her life, she has the power, time, and strength to love others. This is the life of true fulfillment. This is what biblical self-denial is all about: selflessness instead of selfishness, because we are secure in who we are and Whose we are.

Beth Albert was a nurse first in the Philippines and then in China, caring for people with leprosy in the 1950s. Before she became a Christian, someone challenged her by asking, "Beth, you seem one hundred percent for anything you do; wouldn't you like to be one hundred percent for God?" She accepted the challenge.

Six months later she heard about a leprosy clinic that needed nurses. She completed her RN training plus two years of Bible school. After studying leprosy care and treatment, she left for Kunming, China. Here the governor had ordered that, to eliminate leprosy, the military could shoot on sight anyone who appeared to have the disease. As a result, more than 120 people had moved about eight miles out of town to a cemetery, where they were allowed to live. They would sit by the highway and beg in order to survive. Day after day, Beth walked the eight miles to minister to these outcasts of society. She gathered rusting tin cans and taught the people, some of whom did not have fingers, to pack the cans with mud and bake them in the sun to make bricks. From these bricks, they built crude houses to live in. Even after the US Consulate closed because the Communists were taking over China, Beth stayed as long as possible to administer treatment and love.

Writing of her work, Bob Pierce, the founder of World Vision, said,

> *This was the first time these lepers ever had*
> *anybody do anything for them. They were*
> *the most radiant bunch, and they all became*

*Christians. They asked Beth, "Why are you doing this? Nobody ever did anything like this before." And she said, "Because I love Jesus and He loves you. He loves you so much He sent me to help you. You are precious to God and God knows you are beautiful. He knows you are valuable, He sent His Son to earth to die for you so that you might be saved and be in heaven with Him and be in a wonderful place and have a wonderful body. He sent me to show you that He loves you."[30]*

Bob went on to say, "Beth was by all standards the most dauntless, ingenious, level-headed Christian I've ever met; and at the same time, she was the most joyful and the merriest."[31]

God does not want you to *throw* yourself away because you think you're worthless. He doesn't want you to sacrifice yourself to an abusive or destructive relationship. But He does want you to *give* yourself away out of love. This sort of self-denial is rooted

---

[30] Franklin Graham with Jeanette W. Lockerbie, Bob Pierce, This One Thing I Do (Samaritan's Purse, 1983), 70–71.

[31] Ibid.

in true, Christlike self-worth. Because we know our value in God's eyes, we are set free from the trap of selfishness. We are freed to truly love.

## EMBRACING THE WORD

*And he [Jesus] died for all, that those who live should no longer live for themselves but for him who died for them.*
2 CORINTHIANS 5:15

Most people live for themselves. They figure that if they don't take care of themselves, no one else will. Jesus knew that this attitude was a destructive one. It's not only destructive to those around us, it's destructive to ourselves too. It's that same old paradox that Jesus talked about in Matthew 10:39: "Whoever finds their life will lose it, and whoever loses their life for my sake will find it." The very thing we're trying so hard to protect—our own life—will be the thing we end up losing.

But Jesus died so that we could have our lives back again. He shows us the way to real life: a life, that's built on love instead of selfishness. In the end, selfishness leads only to death. But love leads to life both for ourselves and for those around us. Whenever you see a cross during the next few days—on churches or around people's necks—remind yourself that the cross of Jesus Christ reveals to you your true worth. Say a simple prayer in your heart thanking Jesus for His love.

## GOING FURTHER. . .

1. What do these phrases mean to you? Can you personalize them by writing down how they apply to your life in a practical way?

   Deny myself—

   Take up my cross—

   Follow Jesus—

2. How can you apply 2 Corinthians 5:15 (see above) to your own life?

3. In your own words, looking at your own life, what is the difference between a biblical sense of self-worth and self-love?

*God, show me what denying myself means. Help me not to be "too busy with me" to make time for those You want my life to influence, to come away to be with You, and to make time to renew myself.*

# CHAPTER 7

## Secure Enough to Serve

### *Following Christ's Example*

If there was *anyone* who was secure in his identity, wouldn't that be Jesus, Son of God? John 13 shows us His strong sense of identity and self-worth— and His utter humility.

> *It was just before the Passover Festival. Jesus knew that the hour had come for him to leave this world and go to the Father. Having loved his own who were in the world, he loved them to the end. The evening meal was in progress, and the devil had already prompted Judas, the son of Simon Iscariot, to betray Jesus. Jesus knew that the Father had put all things under his power, and that he had come from God and was returning to God; so he got up from the*

*meal, took off his outer clothing, and wrapped*
*a towel around his waist. After that, he poured*
*water into a basin and began to wash his*
*disciples' feet, drying them with the towel that*
*was wrapped around him (John 13:1-5).*

It's amazing to realize that the answers to all
four of those great questions of life we discussed in
an earlier chapter are answered about Jesus in these
few verses.

Jesus knew:

1. Who He was: the Father's Son, with power
   over all things (verse 3).
2. Where He came from: from God (verse 3).
3. Why He was here: to show humanity the full
   extent of His love; to die (verse 1).
4. Where He was going: leaving this world to
   return to the Father (verses 1 and 3).

Even though Jesus knew He was the Son of God,
with power over all things, He washed His disciples'

feet. Foot washing was the task of a servant not a king—a mundane, stinky, messy job in the days of dirt roads and sandals. Even friends left this job to others, and Jesus was certainly more than a friend to His disciples. Still He chose to wash their feet, knowing exactly what that act would demonstrate to them.

Remember, at this time, the disciples were all-too-human men. They often failed to live up to Jesus' expectations of them. Sometimes they doubted, other times they were afraid, and often they were downright stupid. In Mark 9:33–35 we are told that the disciples had a disagreement while walking along the road. While Jesus may not have heard everything they said, He heard enough to confront. "What were you arguing about on the road?" He asked them. "But they kept quiet because on the way they had argued about who was the greatest. Sitting down, Jesus called the Twelve and said, 'Anyone who wants to be first must be the very last, and the servant of all.'"

In washing the feet of His disciples, Jesus

demonstrated not only His own humility and willingness to come as a servant, but how He expected His disciples to live when He was gone from them. They were to live as humble servants, not earthly kings, willing to do the dirty work of life.

Jesus started around the table. He washed the feet of Peter, James, John, Thaddeus, Thomas. . . . But wash the feet of *Judas, the one who would betray Him to the Romans?* Didn't Jesus know that in a few short hours Judas would turn Him over to His enemies and cause His death? Oh, yes, He knew! But Jesus came as the servant of all—even those who would kill Him. By His life and death, He offers cleansing to all—with no exceptions.

What does Jesus' example mean to us in our daily lives? Jesus did not boast about who He was—but how many times have we heard others describe, in great detail, their prestigious, high-paying careers? Jesus never avoided a task that was beneath Him—but how many of us find an excuse not to volunteer in a soup kitchen or a free health clinic? Jesus never downgraded anyone else to make Himself appear better—while we constantly make mental comparisons between us and "them."

And we never read that all the while He was washing their feet, Jesus kept reminding His disciples that He was the Son of God. He didn't say, "This is really not My job, you know." Or, "I hope you're impressed with how humble I am." No, He simply did the job respectfully and lovingly.

A woman who is secure in her identity has this same true freedom to serve others in love. She can perform any task, no matter how humble, and still maintain self-confidence because her sense of self-esteem is not dependent on her rank or position. A woman who exemplified this attitude was Mother Teresa. Willing to care for the filthy, dying poor of Calcutta, India, she displayed the self-esteem of one who didn't care what people thought of her, while caring a great deal about those to whom she ministered. I think we would agree that she was secure in who she was and what she was doing.

As we said in an earlier chapter, this sort of self-worth has nothing to do with either pride or self-love. Instead, it is rooted in humility. "If you are humble," wrote Mother Teresa, "nothing will touch you, neither praise nor disgrace, because you know what you are."[32]

Jesus demonstrated this same humble self-esteem. If He could know who He was and who Judas was and still wash the feet of the one who would soon betray Him, surely I should be able to find the grace and humility to minister to any fellow human being God brings across my path. Think about it. If Jesus could wash Judas's feet, can I say no if He asks me to do something good for a person I don't like? If I have the attitude of Jesus, I will be able to perform any task God asks of me.

Yes, it can be difficult to do menial tasks day after day, *women's work*, and not feel that you are being slighted or that you have to do it because you're a woman and no one else will do it. It's hard when those who do "lowlier tasks" are viewed as lowlier workers (and not God's idea at all). There are many seasons to our lives. Whether you have a spouse who actively engages in parenting with you or not

---

[32] Vinita Hampton Wright and Mary Horner Collins, *Women's Wisdom Through the Ages* (Wheaton, IL: Harold Shaw, 1994), 74.

or definitely as a single mom, mothering young children is a season filled with thankless tasks. Your "calling" or purpose in this time of life is no less valuable in God's eyes than any other season in which you are accomplishing "important" things in the eyes of your culture.

Even in seasons of "service," there are times when it's okay to say *no*. It's necessary to say no. Jesus did not heal every sick person in His world. He didn't feed every hungry person. At times, He walked away from the clamoring crowds.

We can perform any task God calls us to, and we don't need to put ourselves down to others to be humble. Several years ago an American family moved next door to a Chinese woman. Wanting to be friendly, the Chinese lady made a plate of dumplings and took them to her new neighbor. As she gave them to her, the Chinese lady commented, "They're no good!" After the lady left, the American took her at her word and threw them out. A few weeks later the Chinese lady again took dumplings to her new neighbor with the comment, "They're no good!" Again the American threw them out, but this time her curiosity was aroused. After inquiry into Chinese culture, she learned that in old Chinese culture it was considered polite to discredit a gift when presenting it. Similarly, if someone should comment that you have a very fine son, the proper old Chinese response was, "He is really very dumb!"

But when we do this in our culture, we're merely drawing attention to ourselves. Author Hannah Whitall Smith cautioned against this tendency: "Some people think they are humble and lowly in heart when they say bitter and disparaging things about themselves, but I am convinced that the giant ME is often quite as much exalted and puffed up by self-blame as by self-praise."[33]

A friend compliments you about the top you're wearing. What's your first reaction? "Oh, I got this for five dollars at a yard sale." When will we learn that a simple thank-you is the best response? We tend to put ourselves down. Jesus never did that. He never denied who He was. He didn't boast about it, but neither did He ever deny it. He was secure in who He was.

---

[33] Melvin E. and Hallie A. Dieter, *GOD Is Enough* (Hong Kong: Zondervan, 1994).

No one can say Christ denied His divinity. On the other hand, none can say, "I am so low that He did not identify with me." Fully understanding who He was, Jesus did not act in an egotistical way, distancing Himself from people. He limited the expression of Himself while in no way denying His "personhood"—who He really was.

Can we stop putting ourselves down? We can to the degree to which we allow the Holy Spirit to control our decisions and our actions. To do so, we must have a clear sense of who we are—people of value in God's sight—and a willingness to serve others, no matter how humble the task. We can follow in His footsteps.

Of course, we are going to veer off the Jesus path with our own great ideas. We still want to do things our way. Every day we must deal with our selfishness and with the tendency to argue over the details. "Wouldn't this other path be a little quicker?" we might say, or "It's getting dark. Can't we go home yet?" We often get in our own way and sometimes lose sight of Jesus, who is always walking ahead of us and showing us the path we need to take. But when we remember that Christ lives within us and that we can call on Him moment by moment for help, we come closer to His example. Our natures fight hard against living this kind of life, because we are selfish, but as believers we also have Christ living out His life within us.

That attitude puts self-esteem in its rightful place, in a biblical perspective. There is no room for either putting ourselves down or egotism. We can't say, "I'm no good—I will never accomplish anything important," because God has said we are people of value. He has work for us to do for Him. Neither can we say, "I'm too important to lower myself to do that," because Jesus gave us an example by doing the lowliest of tasks for the lowliest of people.

What security! God loves us, and He has laid hold of our lives for a reason. Day by day as we cooperate with Him, we can accomplish the purpose He has for our lives because we are of value to Him.

*In your relationships with one another, have the same mindset as Christ Jesus: Who, being in very nature God, did not consider equality with God something to be used to his own advantage (Philippians 2:5–6).*

Jesus neither boasted about nor put down who He was either in His own thinking or His expression of Himself to others. He was God, and He knew it; He never denied His own nature or attributes. It is a false sense of humility (or is it actually pride?) that makes us think we must deny anything nice someone says about us.

Jesus was willing to come to us on our own level—without sin but with the limitations of humanity. In Philippians 2:7–8 Paul continues by telling us that Jesus gave up His divine privileges, taking the humble position of a slave when he appeared in human form and humbly obeyed God even though it meant that he would die like a criminal by crucifixion on a cross.

If you were setting those phrases to music, each would be in a lower tone than the previous one, but the intensity of each phrase would build because each thought is even more amazing than the previous one!

Christ's work here on this earth was to bridge the gulf between God and sinful humanity. He Himself became that bridge. Although our task is not the same as Christ's, we are urged in Philippians 2:5 to have the same mindset He had toward His life work, namely to:

1. Know and accept who we are—sinners saved by grace and now accepted in Christ, justified, forgiven, adopted into His family, redeemed, cleansed, and in fellowship with God.
2. Be willing to identify with any other human being for whatever purpose God may have for that relationship.

First Corinthians 2:16 says that "we have the mind of Christ." When we follow Philippians 2:5, we will truly have the same "mind" as Jesus. His spirit of love and humility will control our lives.

## EMBRACING THE WORD

*Come near to God and he will come near to you.*
JAMES 4:8

A baby becomes secure in her parents' love by spending time all day long close to these people who love her so much. We too will become secure as we spend more time with God. Set aside some special time, no matter how short, for being alone with God. And then go even further. Talk to Him throughout your day—at work, while you're driving, at home doing housework, wherever you are, whatever you are doing. He is always with you. Make a habit of including Him in your day. When you do, His love will begin to push your fear out the door of your heart.

## GOING FURTHER. . .

1. In your own words, explain how putting yourself down all the time can really be just another form of selfishness. Do you see this in your life?

2. If you were totally secure in God's love, how would you live differently than you do today?

*Jesus, help me to have the same healthy sense of self-worth that You had when You lived on our earth. I don't want to be ruled by selfishness anymore. I want to be ruled by Your love.*

# CHAPTER 8

❧

## Trash or Treasure?

### For Survivors of Abuse

One out of every three women worldwide has experienced either physical and/or sexual violence at some point in their lives.[34] The wounds from this go deep: "We are whole beings. We are body, soul, spirit, mind. We are not just a body or just a mind or just emotions, and damage happens in every level of our being,"[35] explains sexual abuse survivor Kay Warren. A feeling of shame going back to a woman's earliest memory drives her to self-hatred becoming such an integral part of her personality that she thinks that's just the way things are.

Abuse can be physical, sexual, verbal, or

---

[34] "Facts and Figures: Ending Violence against Women," UN Women, November 2018, http://www.unwomen.org/en/what-we-do/ending-violence-against-women/facts-and-figures.

[35] "'Jesus Cares for Our Pain': Beth Moore, Rick and Kay Warren Tell Sex Abuse Victims How They Can Find Healing in Church," CBN News, February 13, 2018, https://www1.cbn.com/cbnnews/us/2018/february/jesus-cares-for-our-pain-beth-moore-rick-and-kay-warren-tell-sex-abuse-victims-how-they-can-find-healing-in-church.

emotional. Words alone can be powerfully devastating. Elizabeth Smart was fourteen when she was abducted at knifepoint from her bed in the middle of the night in Salt Lake City, Utah. Her family searched for her in vain. Nine months later she was recognized while walking down a street with her abductor.

For some time, Smart was kept chained to a tree. Eventually, chains became unnecessary to keep her from fleeing. Words were enough. Her captor constantly threatened to kill her family if she did not comply with his sexual demands. "I have been chained up with actual chains but I have also been chained with words and I can tell you that words are so much stronger than actual chains," she later recounted.[36]

If you are a survivor of abuse, held captive by shame, we have good news for you: Jesus wants to set you free! What's more, He has the power to do it.

In his book *As Jesus Cared for Women*, Dr. W.

[36] "Elizabeth Smart Says Kidnapper Was a 'Master at Manipulation,'" NPR, October 8, 2013, http://www.npr.org/2013/10/08/230204193/elizabeth-smart-says-kidnapper-was-a-master-at-manipulation.

David Hager talks about the woman who washed Christ's feet with her tears. (You can read the story for yourself in Luke 7.) Likely this woman had been wounded by men many times in her life. She had been treated like an object so often that she thought of herself that way too. She no doubt felt worthless.

How amazed she must have been when she met Jesus! Here was a Man who saw *her*—not an object. And He not only saw her, He loved her and forgave her. No wonder she cried as she poured perfume on Jesus' feet. "Perhaps she had cried herself to sleep on many lonely nights," writes Dr. Hager. "Maybe she had cried in pain. . . . On this night, though, she was pouring out to Jesus a lifetime of pent-up guilt and anguish."[37]

Some of us have deeper scars than others, but we all have scars. Dr. Hager writes,

> *When someone hurts us, abandons us, or*
> *embarrasses us, we decide that we will do*
> *whatever it takes never to let that happen*

[37] W. David Hager, As Jesus Cared for Women (Grand Rapids, MI: Revell, 1998), 87.

*again, making subconscious vows to guard the most vulnerable parts of ourselves.*

*These vows may lead us to behaviors that are evil or socially unacceptable before we experience forgiveness or that are self-protective even after we have come to know Christ's love. Yet, He is always ready to help us denounce those vows and to break down those walls that are really barriers to the inner healing God wants to do in our lives. He desires to care for our wounds, and He will, as we are willing to open ourselves to Him and to His loving ministry in our lives.*[38]

As you read the stories in this chapter, remember: If you too have deep wounds from an abusive past, Jesus wants to heal those wounds. He loves you. You are more precious to Him than you could ever imagine.

There is no doubt about it: Rachel was a victim. The word *dysfunctional* hardly begins to describe her family. While her mom was pregnant with Rachel,

---

[38] Ibid, 93.

her dad stabbed her in the stomach, trying to kill his unborn child. Her parents were teenagers, both deaf and unemployed. A divorce soon followed, and Rachel and her mother went to live with her grandparents and two uncles who were only four and five years older than Rachel. The boys taunted Rachel endlessly, locking her out of the house, laughing at her cries for help, which her mother, being deaf, could not hear, and threatening her with violence if she "told" on them. Her grandmother ruled the household with an iron hand, giving orders for beatings to be carried out by an older uncle if she was not obeyed.

When she was about five, Rachel's teenage uncles began to make sexual advances. Stopping at nothing in order to humiliate her, they didn't hesitate to beat her or burn her if she resisted. When more relatives moved into the small house, Rachel was forced to share a bed with one of these uncles.

Rachel enjoyed attending church and developed a love of God at an early age. She was still a child when her mother died after a series of strokes. After her mom's death, her grandmother grudgingly allowed Rachel to continue to live with her.

The family moved to another town, and life improved for Rachel but only for a short time. She was nine now, and because her grandmother was working again, she was required to do the washing, ironing, and cleaning in addition to going to school. Housecleaning included scrubbing the floorboards with a toothbrush and washing every wall, cupboard, and window each week—and she would be sorry if a job wasn't done right! Once when a pot lid wasn't put on properly, her grandma flew into a rage, grabbed all the pots and pans, and threw them on the floor, along with the silverware, canned goods, plastic ware, cereal, and spices. Then she said, "I'm leaving. I expect this kitchen cleaned up spic-and-span or else you've had it when I return!"

Soon alcohol became a problem in the home. Grandma's parties often meant that Rachel was required to bartend, dance, and, of course, clean up afterward. It was no better when her grandmother went out to bars, for then the boys abused Rachel with abandon. Sometimes when her grandmother had drinking debts, she would make deals with the men to whom she owed money and send Rachel to them. Depressed by the effects of alcohol, Rachel's grandmother attempted to drown herself in the toilet, threatened to kill herself with a butcher knife, and tried to jump from a car as it sped down the highway.

Because Rachel was a ward of the state, there was a social worker who visited her home about once a year. Rachel's grandmother turned on the charm during these visits, serving coffee and cookies, and being a gracious hostess. Rachel was too scared to talk. After her grandmother told the social worker what a fine girl Rachel was, the social worker would tell Rachel how lucky she was to have such a wonderful grandma with whom to live.

You may wonder why Rachel didn't ask for help. Actually, one of the priests to whom she went for confession questioned her about what was going on, but Rachel had been so beaten into submission that she blamed herself. She admitted some of the terrible sins she had taken part in at home, and the priest merely told her "not to do it again." Being beaten into the ground was Rachel's normal. The shame in asking for help would have been overwhelming. She doubted if anyone would even believe her.

By now Rachel didn't care about her grades at school; fluent in profanity and shoplifting, she joined a gang. At the same time, she was becoming an excellent dancer. Her ballet teacher, Joyce, became an influence in her life; life at home was a nightmare, but life at Joyce's was Rachel's ray of hope. She made excuses to spend more and more time at her teacher's home. When Rachel shared with Joyce just a little of what was going on, it was so terrible that Joyce was hesitant to believe her. But one day, because of bruises she saw on Rachel, Joyce asked permission to call her social worker. In addition, she invited Rachel to come live with her. For the first time, Rachel felt as if she had a choice, but she was torn. She loved Joyce, and strange as it may seem, she loved her grandmother too.

After a physical fight with her uncles, Rachel walked the fifteen miles to Joyce's home. It was a landmark day for Rachel in more than one way, for on this day Joyce sat down with her and with an open Bible explained how to have a personal relationship with Jesus. For the first time, Rachel heard a clear explanation of the Gospel, and her heart ached for more. Joyce would not pray with her to accept Jesus that day, however. She wanted to be sure it was Rachel's own decision, not one made merely to please her.

The meeting that followed with the social worker resulted only in the social worker saying, "It's your word against your grandmother's, and they will never believe you." When her grandmother learned Rachel wanted to leave home and live with Joyce and that she had told the social worker that her grandma had an alcohol problem, she went into a rage and began to slap Rachel and beat her mercilessly with a belt. "Jesus, help!" was all that Rachel could say over and over. Then, Rachel says, a miracle occurred.

Grandma dropped the belt, began to cry, and said, "I can't hurt you. I love you even though you've stabbed me in the heart."

For the next few weeks, until Rachel left home

for good, life was a nightmare of trying to placate her grandmother. One night during this time, her grandma was drinking extra heavily and was her old raging self, taking her anger out on Rachel.

"I went into Grandma's room and, sitting on the edge of her bed, I prayed a prayer like I never prayed before," Rachel said. "Dear God, if I can know You like Joyce said and You care like Joyce said, I ask You to get me out of this house and let me live with Joyce. If You do, I'll give You my life."

"You are dead to me," her grandmother cried, "and I don't want to remember you ever again, and no one can even speak your name." Rachel watched in horror as her grandmother ripped her baby pictures out of their frames and threw them on the floor at her feet. "You're not welcome here. Get out of my sight!"

Rachel said to me, "I told Grandma I loved her and said goodbye." There was no response.

"When I arrived at Joyce's, she had baked me a cake." In addition, she had bought Rachel a bed and had it all made up for her. It was the beginning of a new life.

When asked what gave her the courage to go on, Rachel said, "It is the Lord who gets me through. He is my Strength, my Sustainer, my Rock, and my Shield. I know I could never make it through without knowing who God is. I pored over Scripture," Rachel went on. "I read in 2 Peter that God has given us 'all things that pertain to life and godliness.' With that Scripture I presented my petition to the Lord and asked for help. I saw through Scripture that God is sovereign. He loves me unconditionally, totally, completely. God is love. When I felt like God didn't care, I knew that was a lie. Scripture tells me He cared deeply and tenderly for the lost, the crippled, the little children. Scripture also says He is 'the same yesterday and today and forever.' So what I read in the Word was the truth; what I felt was a lie. That doesn't mean God doesn't care how I feel, but He also wants me to learn to trust Him."

When the old feelings of shame try to creep in, Rachel is ready.

"I begin by saying the Scriptures. Sometimes I tell myself these truths a thousand times a day until I begin to believe them in my heart. I put them up all over the walls of my house, because I know the battle is fought in my mind: 'Trust in the LORD with all your heart, and lean not on your own understanding; in all your ways acknowledge Him, and He shall direct your paths' [Proverbs 3:5–6 NKJV]. 'Casting all your care upon Him, for He cares for you' [1 Peter 5:7 NKJV]. 'If you, then, though you are evil, know how to give good gifts to your children, how much more will your Father in heaven give good gifts to those who ask him!' [Matthew 7:11]. In Jeremiah the Lord asks, 'Is anything too hard for me?' [Jeremiah 32:27]. His arm is not short that He can't reach me, nor is His ear deaf that He cannot hear. This is what gets me through."

Like many victims, Rachel found that when God was all she had, God was enough.

"My problems were too big for anyone, especially a little girl. I had to take a chance on God. When I prayed that prayer of desperation, 'God, if You let me live with Joyce, I will give You my life,' I only had God to turn to. Now I'm learning to fulfill my end of the deal. I offered my life, and what the Lord gave back is unbelievable—peace, comfort, understanding, joy, and always love. I would never trade my life with the Lord for anything, no matter how hard life gets or how difficult the circumstances are. Whatever I go through is nothing compared to what the Lord went through for me. He is using my experiences to change me, mold me, and shape me, so I will be ready to spend eternity with Him. How can I complain about that? We need an eternal perspective."[39]

Yes, Rachel was a victim. Nearly every one of the important people in her early life let her down. They treated her like trash. With a childhood like this, you would think that it would be impossible for her to realize her great value to God. Yet God is in the business of salvaging lives. Today Rachel is the wife of a pastor, a loving man who understands the damage that has been done in her past, and she is the mother of three. She understands and encourages other women who also are survivors of abuse. Someday she says she'll write a book that she wants to title *Life Is Hard—But God Is Good!*

---

[39] Personal written interview with Darlene Sala, 1999.

Kayla shared about her feelings of worthlessness. She was raised in a home where she was constantly told, "You can't do anything right—you'll never make it!" These discouraging, defeating words sunk down into her soul and her spirit. Kayla said, "Trying hard to win affirmation and to feel really good about myself, I tried all kinds of behavior, sincere and insincere."

Even after she had married a good man and had two daughters, a longing remained in her heart to feel worthwhile to herself and others. She turned to a religion that taught her to think only positive thoughts, but that brought only further slavery, for now she had to prove herself in a different way—by being constantly positive. No one can be genuinely positive all the time, and so her religion forced her to once again deny her true self.

When Kayla was in her thirties, a close friend introduced her to Jesus. "She urged me to read the Bible and to open my heart to Him about my feelings. In my yearning to learn more about my Savior, I found the Bible verse that says, 'See what great love the Father has lavished on us, that we should be called children of God! And that is what we are!' (1 John 3:1).

"This thought awakened my heart with a jolt! I realized I was the daughter of the Lord of lords and King of kings, His child forevermore. The change in my heart began. I was of real value to Him! I experienced a release from the bondage of having to prove myself and having to strive for self-esteem. I was chosen by God to bear fruit for Him. What an awesome privilege for my life."

Victory is never constant, Kayla relates, but in those times of defeat, she repeats, "I am His child," each and every day. Restored again by His love and forgiveness, she can serve Him with a truly grateful heart. No longer looking to others for her feelings of worth, she instead uses that energy to live her days with Jesus out of a heart secure in His love and in joy.

Maybe you feel like trash because the significant people in your life have told you that's what you are and have treated you like it. Don't believe it! You are not your abuse. Nor was the abuse your fault. Not back then, not now, not ever.

Bible teachers Beth Moore and Kay Warren, both survivors of childhood sexual abuse, give six steps all abuse victims must take toward healing. They include:

**1. Establish safety**—Find someone in the church or elsewhere whom you can confide in.

**2. Choose to face the truth and feel**—Admit the gravity of the situation and allow yourself to feel the painful emotions that come with it.

**3. Tell your story**—Telling others can bring healing because it allows others to rally around you in support, and it shows other abuse victims they are not alone. A Christ-centered program like *Celebrate Recovery* can help you heal and know that you are not alone!

**4. Identify the distortions and reclaim God's original design**—Realize the lies about your body, emotions, God, or your self-worth that you have believed. Instead, believe what God has spoken over you.

**5. Repent of deadness and denial**—God has created us to feel, and victims of abuse sometimes deaden their emotions to avoid feeling the pain that has been inflicted on them. Instead, allow yourself to feel those emotions.

**6. Mourning the loss and daring to hope—** Mourn what you have lost, and dare to hope that God will restore what has been stolen from you.[40]

If you are a survivor of any kind of abuse in the past, study this book carefully. Look up each scripture in your Bible and mark it. If you are being abused right now, please get help. You are God's child, and you do not deserve to live in fear. If you are married with children and have an abusive husband, you must protect yourself and your children by putting space between you and your abuser. He needs to take ownership of his problem and get help. And it is *his* problem. Don't believe him when he says it's all your fault and you deserve to be punished, because that's not true. You are a person of value, no matter what he tells you. Go to your pastor or

---

[40] "'Jesus Cares for Our Pain': Beth Moore, Rick and Kay Warren Tell Sex Abuse Victims How They Can Find Healing in Church," CBN News, February 13, 2018, https://www1.cbn.com/cbnnews/us/2018/february/jesus-cares-for-our-pain-beth-moore-rick-and-kay-warren-tell-sex-abuse-victims-how-they-can-find-healing-in-church.

find a shelter, friend, or relative who will take you in temporarily. Go to the police and ask for a restraining order. It won't be easy to do these things. After years of abuse, you will need help from others to say "enough." It may take several attempts, but with support, you can get out of the vicious cycle that is ruining your life and the lives of your children.

If you are a young woman still in school and feel you are being abused, first talk to the uninvolved parent. If that doesn't stop the abuse, talk to your teacher, school nurse, principal, or pastor. Don't be embarrassed. This happens to women all around you, and people may already suspect something is wrong in your family.

You are not in this alone. You can ask God to help you find a way out.

> *[Jesus said:] "The Spirit of the Lord is on*
> *me. . . .He has sent me to proclaim*
> *freedom for the prisoners. . .to set*
> *the oppressed free" (Luke 4:18).*

The Bible also says that the Holy Spirit is the

Helper of the believer in Jesus. He is called "another advocate to help you and be with you forever" (John 14:16). His work is to come alongside you. He can remind you of God's promises and "guide you into all the truth" (John 16:13). He can bring healing to your mind, body, and spirit.

Some of us have suffered at the hands of those who were supposed to love, protect, and guide us. In Alma Kern's book *You Are Special*, she writes:

> *Some of us were born to parents who wanted us and rejoiced at our birth. They received us joyfully as precious gifts from God. They raised us as best they could.*
>
> *Others seem to have been biological accidents, arriving unplanned, unexpected, unwelcomed, and unloved.*
>
> *No matter what the circumstances of your birth, you are not just a happenstance of nature. God made you! God uses the best intentions of people. He can also overrule the worst intentions to accomplish His purpose.*
>
> *You are special. God made you.*[41]

---

[41] Alma Kern, *You Are Special* (St. Louis, MO: Lutheran Women's Missionary League, 1985).

# EMBRACING THE WORD

*He was despised and rejected by mankind, a man of suffering, and familiar with pain. Like one from whom people hide their faces he was despised, and we held him in low esteem.*

ISAIAH 53:3

If you have been rejected and abused by the people closest to you, you're not alone; Jesus understands your pain. He too knew what it was like to be rejected and hated; He knew how much it hurt to have people turn away and ignore your pain. He was the Son of God; He was there when the world was created; and He loved human beings so much that He came to earth to take away their sins. But the people He loved didn't want Him. Humanity rejected Him. They went even further and tortured Him and spit on Him. In the end, they killed Him.

Sometimes when we're hurt, we look at the rest of the world, and it seems like everyone else is happy and loved. We feel that no one else would understand our lives. But Jesus understands. We can pour out our pain and anguish to Him for He has truly "been there." The Bible says, "For God made Christ, who never sinned, to be the offering for our sin" (2 Corinthians 5:21 NLT). That's why Jesus faced rejection and pain: because He loved you so much.

Matthew 21:42 says of Jesus: "The stone the builders rejected has become the cornerstone; the Lord has done this, and it is marvelous in our eyes."

You too may have been rejected by people. The ones closest to you may have made you feel as though you were completely worthless. Your life is like a bunch of broken rubble, ready to be swept into the trash.

But God has other plans for you. He wants to give you the beautiful mansion He is building. Jesus Christ, the same one humanity turned away from, is the cornerstone of that incredible home—and He has a place for you too, a place only you can fill. You are not trash but a precious stone, one of God's treasures.

Isaiah 54:11–12 says, "Afflicted city, lashed by storms and not comforted, I will rebuild you with stones of turquoise, your foundations with lapis lazuli. I will make your battlements of rubies, your gates of sparkling jewels, and all your walls of precious stones."

When you look at your life now, you may see only smashed and broken pieces lying in the dirt. But God sees lapis lazuli and rubies and sparkling jewels. Put your life in His hands, and one day you will shine.

## GOING FURTHER. . .

1. What experiences in your life have made you feel like you are worthless?

2. Have you ever shared these experiences with anyone? It's been said that you are only as sick as your secrets. Is it time you found someone to help you finally face them?

3. Our minds are like computers: When the same message is input over and over, we become programmed to think the same thoughts over and over until they become a part of who we are. If you have been the victim of some form of abuse, your mind has been programmed with lies that say you have no value, that you are unlovable and worthless. You may need

help reprogramming your mind; you may need to work with a counselor or a loving friend. But there is something you can do as well: You can begin to input new messages just as Rachel did, by reading the Bible over and over.

4. Write down one of the verses from this chapter that speaks especially to you. Now read it over and over until you have memorized the main idea. You may want to copy it over on note cards and paste them around your house, in your car, in your purse. Whenever you catch yourself beginning to repeat that old, lying mental program, instantly turn to your verse. Read it over. Say it to yourself. You will be reprogramming your mind with love and truth.

4. Pray for other women who have experienced the same pain you have. Ask God to give you opportunities to reach out and help. When pain is shared, it is always easier to bear.

*God, You know all about the ways I've been hurt. When I felt so alone and unwanted, You were actually right there with me, grieving with me, hurting with me. You loved me from the very beginning. You chose me. I am not garbage. Dear Lord, please heal me. I put myself in Your hands, all the scarred and broken pieces. Use me as You build Your kingdom. I want to shine for You. Amen.*

# CHAPTER 9

## If Only I Hadn't...

### *Living Free of the Past*

"I wish I could believe what you said tonight is really true," the woman commented to the speaker at the close of the service. He had spoken of God's forgiveness, but the deep sadness in her eyes revealed that she had been unable to accept the truth of the message.

With tears filling her eyes, she added, "What I have done is so bad that I can't ever forgive myself!" She felt justified in punishing herself for the rest of her life and was wracked with guilt. The guilt and the thought of those she had hurt by her wrongdoing robbed her of any joy life might bring her way. She was miserable and felt she deserved to live this way.

Megan sat in the circle of women, head in her hands. "I had two abortions," she sobbed. "And then

I lived with my boyfriend in my addiction for so many years and now it's too late. I'll never have children." And the hearts of the other women in the room ached with her, for almost all of them had also experienced anguish over an abortion.

We have all done things we regret. We are sometimes hurtful, quick to betray, or rebellious. We blurt out scathing words in a rush of anger, unable to keep them to ourselves, cutting others to the core. We act unwisely, and others share the consequences.

Then we realize what we have done. "Why did I do that? If only I hadn't said that! I wish I could take it all back." Guilt rushes in when we realize that there are some words and actions that can never be taken back, no matter how they haunt us. The damage has been done.

Even if those we have hurt forgive us, sometimes it seems impossible for us to forgive ourselves, and our lives are permanently marked by guilt, as with the woman above. When someone says she cannot forgive herself, she needs to understand two concepts.

1. Forgiving yourself is not the same thing as saying, "It's okay. What I did wasn't really so bad after all." Sin, no matter who commits it, is wrong. It is an act that affects us and those around us. Ultimately, it is an act against God. We can never whitewash sin. All the rationalizing in the world can't change the fact that sin is wrong.

Many of us, though, have the idea that if we forgive someone (including ourselves), we must say, "What you did is okay. Let's just forget about it and not talk about it anymore." Wrong. Forgiveness does not mean saying that *wrong* is *right*. Neither does it mean saying that the wrong didn't matter. It did matter. It hurt.

What forgiveness *does* mean is that when I forgive, I give up my right to hurt you (or myself) because you hurt me. The sinful act was wrong both in the sight of human beings and in the sight of God, but God has made possible a way of forgiveness that will settle the problem of sin. While it is wrong to commit sin, it is also wrong to continue to punish yourself for sin that God has forgiven. That leads to the second concept.

2. God will forgive you, and if He forgives you, who are you to refuse to forgive yourself? Remember, God is the Creator of our entire reality, so if He says that you are no longer guilty, then that is what is real. If you cling to your guilt, you are clinging to a ghost, a shadow of something that no longer exists. You may continue to be haunted by your guilt your whole life; this awful ghost may rule your life, keeping you from experiencing the joy God wants for you. But you don't have to live that way. God sent Jesus so that guilt would have no more power over you. Don't cling to something that's now only an illusion. God's love and power and forgiveness are real.

Nicole was born when her parents were in their forties. When she was only four, her father died, leaving behind his wife and four children. Nicole was taken to church and given a foundation of faith that later turned out to be indestructible. Then her mother remarried, this time to an alcoholic. Nicole's home life changed drastically. Becoming bitter and resentful, Nicole blamed her parents and God for her unhappiness.

At sixteen, Nicole left home. She searched for love and an end to her inner pain through drugs, alcohol, and a relationship. She was anorexic and suicidal. After a fight with her boyfriend, scared, hopeless, and alone—with a bottle of migraine pills in her hand—she took a desperate, drastic step. The next thing she knew, she was waking up to her stomach being pumped. Her roommate had found her in time. A week later, she discovered she was pregnant. When her boyfriend gave her the ultimatum, "It's me or the baby," she chose the baby, and in a few months the frightened teenager gave birth.

As a new mother, Nicole went back to church and read the Bible, but it was a shallow effort. She still carried the guilt and shame of her failures within her. She had not accepted God's complete forgiveness in her life. With her deep need to feel accepted, she went from one bad relationship to another. Then her life was ripped apart at the seams. She was raped—not by a stranger but by someone she trusted. "I was so full of hurt, anger, shame, and guilt," recalls Nicole, "that I couldn't even pray for help. The truth was, I was afraid to pray. I felt I was

believer yet, and it wasn't until their daughter was born that Justin softened to the idea of going to church. They began to attend casually. Another surprise followed—Nicole was again pregnant, this time with twin girls. Soon they had five young children.

Nicole's life was better in some ways, but her troubles weren't over. She developed throat cancer and went through surgery and radiation. Six months later, her oldest son nearly died from a very painful and never-diagnosed disease.

By now God had Justin and Nicole's undivided attention! When a friend invited them to church, God used Justin's interest in music to draw them in. Now they both have personal relationships with Jesus. Justin plays in the church band, even though it means a long drive from where they live. Nicole is using her life experiences to counsel and teach pregnant teens.

"I have learned not to blame others for my pain but instead realize that it is my choices that put me in these positions; I am responsible. Now, forgiveness has come to my life!" One of her favorite verses is, "Praise be to. . .God. . .the Father of compassion and the God of all comfort, who comforts us in all our troubles, so that we can comfort those in any trouble with the comfort we ourselves receive from God" (2 Corinthians 1:3–4).

Nicole would tell you that no matter how deep into sin you have fallen, no matter how your life is scarred from the results of your choices, God is all about forgiveness and redemption.

Jack Hayford points out that in the ancient Roman world, the word *Corinthian* meant "rotten to the core." The city of Corinth, located in present-day Greece, was known for its sin. In Paul's first letter to the Christians of Corinth, he lists some pretty bad characters: the sexually immoral, idolaters, male prostitutes, homosexual offenders, thieves, the greedy, drunkards, slanderers, and swindlers. He personalizes it when he adds, "And that is what some of you were."

But Paul goes on to declare, "But you were washed, you were sanctified, you were justified in the name of the Lord Jesus Christ" (1 Corinthians 6:11). It would be wonderful enough to be washed, sanctified, and clean. But in his second letter to the Corinthians, Paul adds an even more astounding thought when he writes, "I am jealous for you with a godly jealousy. I promised you to one husband, to Christ, so that I might present you as a pure virgin to him" (2 Corinthians 11:2).

Says Pastor Hayford,

> *Do you hear that, dear one? A chaste virgin. Look at this awesome new creation statement in God's Word! See how former sin and sex addicts are now being declared "virginal"! Can you imagine a more towering statement on how vast the possibilities of God's restorative powers are, once He sets about recovering ruined, broken or sin-stained people?* [42]

These truths are amazing!

Matt and Jessica were delighted when God sent healthy, fine sons into their family, yet Jessica longed for a daughter. In the back of her mind, however,

---

[42] Jack W. Hayford, *The Mary Miracle* (Grand Rapids, MI: Baker Publishing Group, 1994), 99.

she kept thinking that God would not give her a girl because of the life she had lived before she became a Christian. She believed that God wouldn't trust her to raise a daughter properly, so that's why He gave her boys. What a lie Satan was using to influence her image of God! Imagine her joy when the third child God sent to their home was a beautiful baby girl. Now Jessica knew that "if anyone is in Christ, the new creation has come: The old has gone, the new is here!" (2 Corinthians 5:17).

This is where your part comes in. God has done the part we couldn't do—paid the price of forgiveness for sins. Now you must be willing not only to accept His forgiveness but to ignore the condemning thoughts that rear their ugly heads in your mind. You must say, "I know God has forgiven this sin, and so I must forgive myself and others."

This, of course, is easier said than done. Every person with some sensitivity feels guilt for their sins. Sometimes they tell themselves, "I couldn't forgive anyone who did that to me! How can I accept God's forgiveness when I've been so evil? It can't be that simple." Yet this same person can forgive the sins of others, even those that affect her personally. It may involve a bit of an emotional struggle, but most of us are basically forgiving people.

So why can't we forgive ourselves? Why do we punish ourselves for years over a mistake that God and the other people involved have long ago forgotten? This refusal to accept God's forgiveness and cleansing is wrong. God has given you the greatest gift He could find, and we tell Him, "No, thanks. I don't believe I'm worthy of it, so please take it back." How would you feel if your kid said that at Christmas? What if your best friend said that when you handed her a birthday present? You wouldn't understand, would you? You'd think *What in the world?* and you'd get angry. "My gift isn't good enough for you? What did you want anyway?" And you might stomp out the door.

No matter how we feel about God's forgiveness, no matter how unworthy we believe we are, if we refuse to accept His forgiveness and choose to listen to Satan, we hurt God deeply.

No sin is so bad that Christ's sacrifice does not atone for it. Do you believe this? Then resist

Satan when he tries to haunt you with the ghosts of your old sins. Accept what God says is true about you. Ask God's Spirit to control your thinking, for "letting the Spirit control your mind leads to life and peace" (Romans 8:6 NLT). Ask God to help you begin to live in the freedom of forgiveness.

Jesus came to our earth because we had all sinned. He came because of *you*. Nothing you have ever done could make Him ever forget about you. Amy Carmichael writes,

> *To me, one of the proofs that God's hand is behind and all throughout this marvelous book we know as the Bible is the way it continually touches upon this very fear in us— the fear that we are so insignificant as to be forgotten. That we are nothing. Unconsciously, His Word meets this fear, and answers it—not always by a direct statement, but often by giving a simple, loving little story.*
>
> *John, looking through the thin veil of time into eternity, saw his Lord—the Lord he had seen pierced—now holding in His hand*

*seven stars. John declares: "I fell at His feet*
*as though dead." Immediately—just as*
*though this fallen one mattered more than*
*the seven stars, as though there were no*
*stars—"He placed His right hand upon me"*
*(Revelation 1:17).*

*Isn't it beautiful that there was no*
*rebuke at all for their human weakness?*
*And there never is a rebuke for our weaknesses*
*either. "The soul of the wounded calls for help,*
*and God does not regard it as foolish"*
*( Job 24:12 EBR).[43]*

You are important to God.

Guilt can be healthy. It can show us what needs to change in our lives. Guilt, however, is not the same thing as shame. Guilt says, "I did something bad (that I need to address with God), but shame says, "I AM bad." Conviction is from God, shame is not. God is offering you the gift of forgiveness through His Son Jesus Christ. All you have to do is reach out and take it.

---

[43] Amy Carmichael, *You Are My Hiding Place* (Minneapolis: Bethany House, 1991).

Corrie ten Boom has a wonderful illustration about how to deal with the past:

> *Guilt is a useful experience because it shows where things are wrong. It is dangerous when it is not there at all, just as the absence of pain when someone is ill can be dangerous.*
>
> *When we belong to Jesus we are not called to carry our guilt ourselves. God has laid on Jesus the sins of the whole world. What you have to do is to tell Him everything, confess your guilt and sin and repent, and then He will cleanse you and throw all your sins into the depths of the sea. Don't forget there is a sign that reads "No fishing allowed."*[44]

## EMBRACING THE WORD

*A Chain of Forgiveness*

Here's what we want you to do. Turn to 1 John 1:9 in your Bible. It's one of the most helpful verses dealing with sin and forgiveness: "If we confess our

---

[44] Corrie ten Boom, *Each New Day* (Grand Rapids, MI: Revell, 1977).

sins, he is faithful and just and will forgive us our sins and purify us from all unrighteousness."

Beside that verse in your Bible, write a reference to Ephesians 1:7: "In him we have redemption through his blood, the forgiveness of sins, in accordance with the riches of God's grace." Now turn to Ephesians 1:7, and beside it write Psalm 130:4, which says, "But with you there is forgiveness, so that we can, with reverence, serve you."

Continue the chain of verses by writing next to that verse Psalm 103:12 (NLT): "He has removed our sins as far from us as the east is from the west." The next verse in the chain is Isaiah 43:25 (NLT): "I— yes, I alone—will blot out your sins for my own sake and will never think of them again." Next to Isaiah 43:25, write Micah 7:19 (NLT): "Once again you will have compassion on us. You will trample our sins under your feet and throw them into the depths of the ocean!"

Take time to write down what each of those verses you listed in the Chain of Forgiveness says about the sin for which you have not forgiven yourself. Confess your sin to God and agree with Him that what you did was wrong. Then remember that it was for your sin that Jesus died on the cross. The good news is that you don't have to catch God in a good mood in order to be forgiven. In fact, please understand that it is not merely because God loves you that He will forgive you. He has promised to forgive you because His Son has already paid the penalty for that sin. You don't owe God for that sinful act. The price has been paid in advance, and you are debt-free once you confess the sin to God and accept His forgiveness.

Have you confessed your sin to Him? Has He forgiven you? The Bible says He will. Believe that He keeps His word, then resist the voice of Satan, who wants to accuse you of the sin for which God has forgiven you. The devil is called "the accuser of our brothers and sisters. . .the one who accuses them before our God day and night" (Revelation 12:10 NLT).

Tammy De Armas works with women in crisis at a crisis pregnancy center in Southern California. She says that right up until the moment a woman has an abortion, Satan whispers in her ear, "This is the best choice. It will solve all your problems!" and the *minute* she has the abortion, he sneers, "What did you do?! What did you do?!"[45]

Yes, Satan loves to torment women. Before he was ejected from heaven by trying to be equal with God, the Bible tells us that Satan was dazzlingly beautiful, "perfect in beauty" (Ezekiel 28:12), adorned with great glory, covered with gemstones. He was the most gorgeous thing God had created—and then he sinned by pridefully thinking he should be equal with God and was thrown out of heaven.

Ever since Eve was created as the crown of creation, beautiful in form and spirit, Satan has been going after her—going after us, instigating oppression and sexual violence in every culture.

But Revelation 12:10 also says that there will be an end to this; someday Satan will be destroyed, but until then we can resist the devil's efforts to defeat us through accusations that are lies, not the truth.

> *"He [Satan] was a murderer from the beginning, not holding to the truth, for there is no truth in him. . .for he is a liar and the father of lies" (John 8:44).*

---

[45] Personal interview June 2019.

*Humble yourselves before God. Resist the
devil, and he will flee from you. Come close
to God, and God will come close to you
(James 4:7–8 NLT).*

*Stay alert! Watch out for your great enemy,
the devil. He prowls around like a roaring
lion, looking for someone to devour. Stand
firm against him, and be strong in your faith.
Remember that your family of believers all
over the world is going through the same kind
of suffering you are (1 Peter 5:8–9 NLT).*

Here's one more thing: since it is Satan's job to try to
get you to doubt God's Word, you probably should
add one more verse to your Chain of Forgiveness, a
verse that does not deal with forgiveness but with
your thought life:

*We destroy arguments and every lofty opinion
raised against the knowledge of God, and take
every thought captive to obey Christ
(2 Corinthians 10:5 ESV).*

# GOING FURTHER. . .

1. Before I can forgive myself or someone else, I must first agree with God that the sin was wrong. If forgiveness doesn't mean just saying, "That's all right; it doesn't matter," what does it mean to really forgive someone (or yourself)?

2. Is forgiveness a fact or a feeling? Explain the difference.

3. What does it mean to you that in 2 Corinthians 11:2 the apostle Paul says believers are "pure virgins"?

4. What does it mean for you to "take every thought captive to obey Christ" (2 Corinthians 10:5)? Give a practical example relating to forgiveness.

*Dear God, sometimes I can hardly believe that You can really love me. I can hide some of my sins and mistakes from others, but I can't hide them from You. You know everything I have ever done. And yet, God, You love me. You loved me so much*

*You sent Your Son to take away my sin. As hard as I try, I can never really comprehend Your love. I can never really grasp that, from Your perspective, all the sins of my past don't even exist anymore. No, I'll never understand Your love and forgiveness. All I can do is say thank You. Amen.*

# CHAPTER 10

*⬥*

## Getting Personal

### *We Struggle Too!*

Have we ever struggled with issues of self-worth, you ask? Absolutely. (Or we wouldn't have written this book!) We all may struggle in different ways, but hope for all of our struggles is found in Him. Here's a bit about each of our personal identity journeys.

## DARLENE:

As I grew up, the people I admired most were extroverts. And I met a lot of them, since my dad was a pastor, and we had outstanding Christian leaders and missionaries in and out of our home constantly. Being an only child, I spent a considerable amount of time listening to adult conversations among my parents and these fascinating people—when I wasn't sitting listening to them speak in church services (I did a *lot* of sitting and listening). They told amazing stories about dodging death by joining in with the natives of Bolivia in their tribal dances—natives who originally planned to kill them. About having rocks thrown at them as they preached in Colombia because they were believers. About speaking to hundreds of people and seeing them make decisions to receive Christ into their lives. And in my mind, they were all extroverts.

I too felt God's call on my life—but I was an introvert. What could He possibly do with me? I had the impression that if you were an introvert, you would never be as important or valuable as the one who was always selected as the leader—the one with the "great" personality and good public speaking ability, the one who never knew a stranger. In my mind, the extrovert was more valuable than the introvert. Yet, is that really true?

To figure it all out, I had first to understand the difference between an extrovert and an introvert. I learned, in simple terms, an extrovert is one who draws her energy from being with people. She may be dog-tired at the end of the day, hardly able to put one foot in front of the other, but she has a party to attend that night, so she reluctantly takes a shower, dresses, and drives to the party. Four hours later, the extrovert, who was so tired she could hardly drag herself there, is one of the last to leave. She is vibrant and full of energy, wide-awake, and charming to the end. Why? Because she draws energy from being with people. Social activity recharges her batteries.

How about the introvert? She too received an invitation to the party. She gets there, enjoys talking intimately with one or two close friends, and thirty minutes later she is wishing she could go home. (How well I know!) The longer the evening goes, the more tired she is. Instead of being recharged by the party, it drains her energy. But the next night she has an evening at home to herself, and she works on plans to redecorate her apartment. The hours slip by until she looks up at the clock and finds it is midnight. Yet she is more revitalized than when she began. She draws her energy from entirely different sources than the extrovert.

It took me a long time to learn that we can never say an extrovert's life is more meaningful than the introvert's; they're just different. While the introvert may wish she were more outgoing in social situations, the extrovert may go home after an event, thinking, "Why did I talk so much tonight? Why can't I keep my mouth shut?"

I'm so glad for extroverts. If it weren't for them, life would certainly be boring. We'd have fewer parties and social events and family reunions. We'd laugh a lot less and be a lot lonelier. On the other hand, I eventually gained new respect for introverts, myself included. I learned to appreciate the gifts God had given me that were different from those of extroverts. I realized that if it weren't for introverts in this world, less scientific research would be done. Intricate art would go unfinished because the extrovert did not have the patience to complete it. Theology books would probably not be compiled. And complex computer programs might never be written because the picky, long-term work of life depends on introverts.

Almost as a surprise to me, being an introvert

has not meant that I could not accomplish significant things with my life. As with many introverts, I have found that putting words on paper is easier for me than speaking—extemporaneous speaking such as being interviewed on a talk show is enough to put me into a mild panic attack! So, my first love has been writing, and that has led to publishing about fifteen books in a number of languages, including Russian, Ukrainian, Spanish, Korean, Uzbek, Indonesian, Albanian, and Chinese. In addition, I host a two-minute weekly radio program translated into several languages and heard in many countries. Who would ever have thought?! I do a weekly blog available on Facebook and by free subscription. And I do enjoy speaking both with my husband for marriage and family conferences and on my own at Bible studies, retreats, and to women's groups. Let me warn you, however, if you are an introvert, you will spend *hours and hours* in preparation for those times of public speaking, because it will be very important to you to think deeply about what you want to say.

But do you want to know a secret? While I love

speaking to various groups, standing around making small talk before and afterward is *painful* for me. Sometimes the only escape at an event has been to retreat to the ladies' restroom just to be by myself and recharge my batteries. There! Now you know the truth. I love all of you; I'd just rather dialog with you one at a time! I may not chatter incessantly, but I'm a good listener.

When it comes to outstanding women in the Christian world, I have a hero I look up to: Elisabeth Elliot, who was a missionary, college professor, and an outstanding speaker and author, and influenced the lives of thousands (see Chapter 6). Yet in a TV interview, she would often answer her interviewer's questions with one-word answers because off-the-cuff, spontaneous speaking was not easy for this highly intelligent and gifted woman, who thought profoundly and wrote prolifically. To me, she is proof positive that God uses introverts.

If I had not been born an introvert, I would never have written the original edition of *Created for a Purpose* as I worked through my issues. The book would not have been in a hospital gift shop when an administrator of the hospital reached up to the top shelf looking for counsel as she contemplated suicide. Neither would it have been on the book rounder at a truck stop when a young girl bought something to read while running away from home with her truck-driver boyfriend. She read halfway through the book and insisted he stop and let her out so her dad could pick her up. Lives turned around!

Being an introvert or extrovert may be a factor in your popularity, but it has nothing to do with your value in God's sight. God made both introverts and extroverts because He has special work for each of us to do. We're each gifted for that work. The apostle Paul reminded us that "each of you has your own gift from God; one has this gift, another has that" (1 Corinthians 7:7). "For we are God's handiwork, created in Christ Jesus to do good works, which God prepared in advance for us to do" (Ephesians 2:10). All He asks is that we put all He has given us, whatever that is, back into His hands.

# BONNIE:

When I was in college, the unthinkable happened. I failed. Well, not exactly as in I got an F in a class. I actually got a B. But I wrote home, "I'm so ashamed of myself. I didn't do my best and I wish I were dead." What really happened to "ruin" my perfect GPA was that I sat in the back row of my Bible class and goofed around (and had fun) because, after all, I was a pastor's kid and a missionary kid and, "Umm. . .yes, I know all about the Bible."

I have been 100 percent guilty of being a perfectionist. A controlling, opinionated perfectionist. We're practicing self-compassion though these days, and with the passing of time, and the work of pain and God in my life, I've come to understand where my need to be "perfect" came from. I also know that I'm not alone in having struggled with this particular issue. Psychologist Dr. David Stoop talks about the "aversion to average that infiltrates every area of our lives."

> *We want the perfect marriage with the*
> *perfect partner. We also want to be perfect*
> *parents who raise perfect kids, who require*
> *nothing from us and do everything right. . . .*
> *Of course, that means we have to be perfect.*

*We want perfect teeth, perfect skin, perfect weight, and perfect health. We dream of a family, a community, a country, and a world at peace—all in perfect harmony.*[46]

I've learned that my drive to be "perfect" had a lot to do with what others thought of me. My sense of self-worth wasn't coming from either within myself or from who God said I was at all. I was trying to please, perform, and perfect so that you would like me, think I was special, and accept me.

My college dorm was part of a set of four high-rises that were connected by a giant lobby filled with sitting areas and surrounded by glass walls. We called it the "fishbowl" because that's where you sat to be seen. Who you were sitting with, especially if a member of the opposite sex, was all-important. People were watching. Having grown up as the kid of parents in ministry and having had to be "on display," I was very comfortable in this environment. I'd grown up in a fishbowl. I made sure I'd straightened my frizzy, curly hair one last time and flicked

---

[46] David A. Stoop, *Living with a Perfectionist* (Nashville: Thomas Nelson, 1987), 49.

on a fresh coat of lip gloss before I showed up in that space. Presentation was *everything*.

This desire to be and have a life that looked "perfect" set me up for putting up with decades of abuse and adultery, looking good on the outside and "faking it" in a twenty-seven-year marriage long after it became clear that I'd made a colossal mistake. More than just a bad habit, my perfectionism also had a devastating impact on those I love.

On the inside, I was hiding a very scared girl who, in the eighth grade, had had to move around the world to a new country and culture quite suddenly. After a few years overseas, cut off completely from my teen culture in the States, I returned to Southern California, feeling like a complete Martian and sure that I looked like one too as I enrolled in a high school of four thousand kids. I didn't know a single one of them. Being cool was out of the question, but I could be perfectly. . .smart!

Shame researcher, Dr. Brené Brown, offers a great definition of perfectionism:

*Perfectionism is a self-destructive and*

*addictive belief system that fuels this*
*primary thought: If I look perfect, live*
*perfectly and do everything perfectly,*
*I can avoid or minimize the painful*
*feelings of shame, judgment and blame.*[47]

She adds: "Perfectionism is an unattainable goal."[48]

Maybe you don't struggle with perfectionism. Maybe you feel like you'll be enough when:

- You lose twenty pounds
- You can get pregnant
- He calls back and asks you out again
- You get/stay sober
- Your kids make you proud
- You finish your degree
- You get that job
- You pay off your debt
- You accomplish that dream

Jesus isn't the one telling us that we need to be perfect or achieve any of the things on that list.

---

[47] Brené Brown, *The Gifts of Imperfection* (Center City, MN: Hazelden Publishing, 2010), 57.
[48] Ibid.

After her decade-long study, talking to thousands of people, Brown said that "One thing separated the men and women who felt a deep sense of love and belonging from the people who seem to be struggling for it. That one thing is the belief in their worthiness."[49]

She asks, "How do we learn to embrace our vulnerabilities and imperfections so that we can engage in our lives from a place of authenticity and worthiness? How do we cultivate the courage, compassion, and connection that we need to recognize that we are enough—that we are worthy of love, belonging, and joy?"[50]

*A deep sense of love and belonging? Engaging in life from a place of authenticity and worthiness?* We so hope that by the time you have reached this point in this book, you perk right up at these words. Because this is exactly what we've been saying that Jesus has made possible for us. We can be uniquely who He created us to be because we can know what our identity, our worthiness, is based on!

[49] Ibid, 23.

[50] Brené Brown: Graduate School of Social Work—University of Houston, April 22, 2019, https://www.uh.edu/socialwork/about/faculty-directory/b-brown/.

Brown urges us to make a "daily practice of letting go of who we think we're supposed to be and embracing who we are."[51] Oh that we would make a daily habit of sitting with Jesus, letting go of who we think we're supposed to be and embracing *who* He says that we are in His love letter called the Bible, and when He gently reminds us *Whose* we are as we listen. Writer Ann Voskamp puts it so clearly: "It is your intimacy with Christ that gives you your identity. When your identity is in Christ, your identity is the same yesterday, today and tomorrow. Criticism can't change it. Failing can't shake it. Lists can't determine it. When your identity is in the Rock, your identity is rock-solid. As long as God is for you, it doesn't matter what mountain rises ahead of you. You aren't your yesterday, you aren't your messes, you aren't your failures, you aren't your brokenness. You are brave enough for today, because He is. And you are enough for all that is, *because He always is.*"[52]

You can live your life from a rock-solid sense of your identity and the assurance that you are worthy,

[51] Ibid.

[52] Ann Voskamp, The Broken Way (Grand Rapids, MI: Zondervan, 2016), 185.

*oh so worthy*, of love, belonging, and joy! Cultivating courage, compassion, and connection are good and helpful things. But they will never be enough to satisfy your longing to be utterly convinced, to know deep within yourself, how much you are loved because you are loved by Him who gave absolutely everything so that you could know and live and breathe in this love. Write these simple truths on your heart:

> "I have loved you *with an everlasting love;*
> *I have drawn you with unfailing kindness*"
> (*Jeremiah 31:3, emphasis added*).

> "*Do not be afraid, for I have ransomed you.*
> *I have called you by name;* you are mine"
> (*Isaiah 43:1* NLT, *emphasis added*).

Will we all feel shame from time to time? Yes. Remember Satan, the father of lies? I like what Brown suggests we do in times of shame: "Don't shrink. Don't puff up. Stand your sacred ground."[53]

---

[53] Brown, *The Gifts of Imperfection*, 53–54.

What makes the ground you stand on sacred is what Jesus has done for you and what He says about you! He says He has loved you, He drew you to Himself with kindness, He has ransomed you, called you, and you are His.

Let's press on! To paraphrase Philippians 3:12: Not that we're already there or already perfect; but we press on, so that we find—we live out—that purpose for which Jesus got ahold of each one of us. We've said that our purpose is to live our real-world, daily lives for God's glory.

Living "for God's glory" or to "bring Him glory" can be a hard thing to grasp. What does that mean for you? For me? Is it a career? Is it some sort of spiritual calling? We've talked about stopping to think about who we are as individuals, our "SHAPE" (Chapter 5, Question 1). Too often we look around at others to try to figure out who we are and what we are supposed to be doing with our lives. Remember, Philippians 3:12 doesn't talk about the reason God got ahold of *all of us*. . .Paul uses the word ME. Your "purpose" will be something that gives you deep satisfaction.

Eric Liddell's story was told in the Oscar-winning film *Chariots of Fire*. Eric was born to run. He was also born to be a missionary to China. Before he won a gold medal in the 1924 Olympics in Paris, his sister urged him to give up running and get on with becoming a missionary—the *more important* work, right? Eric answered her with these words: "God made me fast. And when I run, I feel His pleasure."

God's purpose for you may differ in different seasons of your life. But when you are doing His will, you will feel His pleasure, for you are fulfilling the purpose He created you for.

## WHERE DO I GO FROM HERE?

Here's what the healthy self knows: Yes, you're full of imperfections, gifted in some areas and limited in others. You may or may not appear to be important the way our world rates importance, but you are very valuable to God. He paid a great price to give you forgiveness and to allow you to have relationship with Him through Christ's death on a cross.

If you struggle with your sense of identity, right here and now determine that you are going to do the following:

1. *I will accept Christ's death on a cross as sufficient payment for all my sins.* God promised to forgive you if you confess your sins to Him. Make a conscious decision to trust His Word that the slate has been wiped clean.

2. *I will forgive myself for the mistakes in my past.* Remember that Satan is the one who continually brings old, forgiven sins to your mind. Recognize his attempts to defeat you by accusing you of a wrong for which God has forgiven you, and then resist him in God's strength.

3. *I will accept my worth based on what God says about my value.* Realize that overcoming old patterns takes time as well as determination. When you read the Bible, you build principle upon principle until God's promises become the foundation upon which you base your new life. Always keep in mind that you are a child of God, the daughter of the King (1 John 3:1).

4. *I will settle accounts quickly with God.* When you sin, immediately turn to Him. Admit the awfulness of your sin. Take responsibility for it. Then ask and accept the forgiveness He offers you. If you do this, you won't be burdened by a guilty conscience.

5. *I will determine to lay hold of the purpose He has for my life.* You may not feel that God is using you for any lasting purpose, but decide by faith to trust His promise and wait for the results. There is no distinction between a spiritual "calling" or a vocational career. Our calling, no matter what it is, is spiritual because it comes from the Holy Spirit and speaks to our spirits. For believers, there is no distinction between the "holy" and the mundane. So too living out God's purpose in your life doesn't mean you will be free from problems or even tragedy. Your suffering, however, will not be wasted but will be used by God.

6. *I will refuse to let anyone make me feel inferior, just as I refuse to consider myself to be better than anyone else. By the grace of God, I will be me!*

Remember, you are not a mistake; you are a potential masterpiece. As you put your life in God's hands and really trust Him, He will make you into the unique work of art that He has designed you to be. Only in eternity will you see and understand the completed picture created by God's work in your life.

## ABOUT THE AUTHORS

Darlene Sala lives in Mission Viejo, California. She and her husband, Harold, founded the ministry of Guidelines International, a Christian ministry that shares life-giving devotionals in over fifteen languages throughout the world, on-air and online. Her audio devotional, *Encouraging Words*, may be found at guidelines.org. Darlene writes for women, authoring more than fifteen books. She is a speaker, mother of three adult children, and grandmother of eight, seven grandsons and one princess.

Bonnie Sala also lives in Mission Viejo, California. She leads the ministry of Guidelines as president and is cohost of the *Guidelines for Living* audio devotional on-air and at guidelines.org. Bonnie is an author, speaker, mother of two grown sons and loves nothing more than encouraging women around the world with hope in Christ.

For additional help,
write to Darlene Sala or Bonnie Sala
info@guidelines.org
www.guidelines.org

Guidelines International
26161 Marguerite Parkway, Suite F
Mission Viejo, CA 92692
949-582-5001